THE COMPLETE GUIDE TO
CARING FOR YOUR
DOG

Graham Meadows and Elsa Flint

NEW
HOLLAND

First published in 2004 by New Holland Publishers Ltd

London • Cape Town • Sydney • Auckland

www.newhollandpublishers.com

86 Edgware Rd	80 McKenzie St	14 Aquatic Drive	218 Lake Rd
London	Cape Town	Frenchs Forest	Northcote
W2 2EA	8001	NSW 2086	Auckland
United Kingdom	South Africa	Australia	New Zealand

Publisher: Mariëlle Renssen
Publishing managers: Claudia Dos Santos, Simon Pooley
Senior designer: Geraldine Cupido
Editor: Leizel Brown
Designer: Janine Cloete
Illustrations: Steven Felmore
Picture researcher: Karla Kik
Production: Myrna Collins
Consultant: Rita Davis

ISBN 1 84330 845 2 (paperback)

Reproduction by Hirt & Carter (Cape) Pty Ltd
Printed and bound in Singapore by Kyodo Printing Pte Ltd

Although the author and publishers have made every effort to ensure that the
information contained in this book was correct at the time of going to press,
they accept no responsibility for any loss, injury or inconvenience sustained by
any person using this book.

CONTENTS

DOGS AND PEOPLE 6

A NEW DOG FOR YOU 22

CARING FOR YOUR DOG 34

NUTRITION 48

DOG BEHAVIOUR 62

TRAINING YOUR DOG 72

COMMON BEHAVIOURAL PROBLEMS 86

PROTECTING YOUR DOG'S HEALTH 102

MONITORING YOUR DOG'S HEALTH 124

GROWING OLD 152

BREEDING AND REPRODUCTION 162

CHOOSING A BREED 170

GLOSSARY 186

INDEX 188

PICTURE CREDITS 192

DOGS AND PEOPLE

▶ FROM WILD ORIGINS TO DOMESTICATION ◀

If you have ever thought that Alaskan Malamutes and German Shepherd dogs look very much like wolves, you are pretty close to the mark. Despite many opinions as to exactly how and where our modern dog breeds originated, there is very strong evidence (DNA analysis) that domesticated wolves were their common distant ancestors.

Wolves *(Canis lupus)*, also known as grey wolves, are found only in the northern hemisphere, throughout Europe, North America and Asia. Wolves in the far north vary in colour: animals in a single pack may be black, grey-brown, and white. Those in warmer climates are less aggressive, smaller, and more uniform in colour, often yellowish-fawn or grizzled grey-brown like the domestic dog *(Canis familiaris)*.

Dogs and wolves are both classified as members of the family *Canidae* and share similar characteristics. These are

- 42 teeth
- 50–52 vertebrae (seven cervical, 13 thoracic, seven lumbar, three sacral, 20–22 coccygeal)
- a circularly contracting iris
- a similar sense of smell
- similar diseases
- similar behaviour
- an exceptional sense of direction
- nocturnal habits
- a propensity to dig
- gestation of nine weeks
- the eyes of their puppies open at about two weeks of age.

Above: *Elderly people can benefit greatly from the company of a dog.*
Left: *A distinct bond usually develops between dogs and humans.*

▶ WOLVES AND PEOPLE ◀

We can understand how and why an association developed between wolves and people if we compare their lifestyles during the period of history (between 15,000 and 60,000 years ago) that led to the wolf's domestication.

Humans were semi-nomadic hunter-gatherers. They lived in groups, used natural shelters such as caves and made forays to hunt for food. They had leaders upon whose skill or experience the rest of the group relied. Hunting required physical strength and was primarily the task of males; cooking food and rearing children was largely the domain of females.

Wolves also lived together in extended family groups, or packs, within which there was a distinct hierarchy and a pack leader. They made use of what natural shelter was available, and like humans they also made forays to hunt. Females gave birth to, and reared, their cubs, and for much of the time relied on the strength and ability of the males to protect them and provide food.

Because wolves and humans were hunters, they almost certainly competed with each other from time to time. The wolf's acute sense of smell helped it to track down its prey, and

Above: *Grey wolves in a wild environment – the wolf on the right has adopted a typical greeting posture, while the wolf on the left has been distracted.*

8   DOGS AND PEOPLE

humans may have taken advantage of this by finding wolves that had made a kill, driving them away and taking over the carcass. Wolves probably followed the humans who were hunting and picked up any scraps that were left behind.

As time went by, humans developed a distinct advantage over their canine competitors: the ability to use primitive weapons that made their hunting more effective. A better supply of food meant a more stable lifestyle, and humans began to spend more time in semi-permanent encampments.

Bones from wolf-like dogs have been found in excavations of human encampments dating from 30,000 to 60,000 years ago. They were almost certainly not pets, but semi-wild animals killed by the human inhabitants for food, or had been attracted to the encampments to scavenge on food scraps. Humans may have encouraged such scavengers, for the wolves' superior sense of smell and hearing would have enabled them to detect approaching predators, such as bears or lions, much sooner than the human residents.

Early humans probably made use of the wolf's hunting and scenting ability, and the protection it offered, in much the same way that we use dogs today. In return the wolves obtained some food, and by remaining close to encampments also received a certain amount of protection, for most large predators would not venture too close to humans.

▶ THE PROCESS OF DOMESTICATION ◀

Over a period of time, wolves living close to humans became more relaxed and sociable towards them. Both dogs and humans discovered mutual benefits from this loose association, which gradually became closer and led to the process of domestication. One of the key factors in this process was the wolf's natural instinct to obey a pack leader, and the ability of humans to fulfil that role. Caught when very young, a wild wolf cub was likely to obey its human master and be tamed.

Domestication was a gradual process that occurred during very similar time periods in Europe, Asia and North America – around 10–15,000 years ago. Initially humans used the subspecies of wolf that occurred in their particular area, but as humans migrated there came a great deal of interbreeding.

Four subspecies of wolf had a particular influence on the development of our modern dog breeds:

• The Indian wolf probably gave rise to the ancestors of the Dingo and Asian Pariah Dog. The Dingo's ancestors moved eastwards with human migration, and eventually became isolated in Australia.
• From the Chinese wolf evolved breeds such as the Pekingese and Chow Chow.
• The North American grey wolf was a major source of North American breeds, such as the Eskimo Dog and Alaskan Malamute.
• European wolves were probably involved in the development of breeds such as the various Shepherd Dogs, Spitz types and Terriers we know today.

Inset: *The grey wolf is the ancestor of many North American dog breeds, such as the Eskimo Dog and the Alaskan Malamute.*

PATTERNS OF DOMINANT AND SUBMISSIVE BEHAVIOUR IN WOLVES

DOMINANT BEHAVIOUR		SUBMISSIVE BEHAVIOUR	
Dominant pose	Stiff, tall stance. Ears up or forward. Tail up or out.	Submissive posture	Crouched posture. Ears flat and tail tucked in. Forehead smooth. Pulling corners of mouth back ('grinning'). Licking or extruding the tongue. Lowering and averting gaze.
Feet on	Dominant places its forelegs across the shoulders of a sub-ordinate.	Submissive arched posture	Back very arched and neck curved down and to the side. Head low, muzzle extended up. Tail tucked in and ears flat. Lifting hind leg while dropping to the ground, exposing the inguinal region.
Muzzle pin	Dominant either bites or grabs subordinate's muzzle, forcing it to the ground and keeping it there.	Submissive sit	Sitting back, tucking chin into chest, sometimes pawing at the dominant, and averting gaze.
Stand across	Dominant stands stiffly across the fore-quarters of a prone subordinate.		

▶ THE DEVELOPMENT OF DOG TYPES ◀

The process of selection and refinement lasted many thousands of years, and was based on the human needs for food, protection and companionship. Dogs had an excellent sense of smell and were faster and more agile than men, so they proved to be valuable allies when it came to tracking and hunting the animals on which humans relied for their food, skins and fur. Dogs also proved useful for watch and guard duty, and for killing the vermin that were attracted to the food in the human encampments. Some wolves proved better at certain tasks than others, and human selection gradually produced different types of dog.

During the Neolithic Age, which started about 8000 years ago, humans learned to grow crops. They also domesticated and farmed goats, sheep and cattle, so they selected dogs to provide a further service: herding.

By choosing their primitive domestic dogs for different purposes, humans incidentally selected for particular characteristics. Among these were temperament, body shape and body size.

It is suggested that in selecting for temperament they chose animals that were playful, outgoing and showed little aggression towards people, yet readily barked at the appearance of

intruders. These traits were consistent with the behaviour of young animals, and over a period of time resulted in an adult population that retained many 'puppy' characteristics. Scientifically, this is referred to as 'neoteny'.

In developing a dog type, body shape and size were clearly important. Dogs required to hunt fast-running prey needed speed and agility, and therefore a relatively light, fine-boned body with long legs and a flexible spine. Large, strong dogs were required to hunt prey such as gazelles, but dogs used for hunting hares could be smaller. A dog whose main job was to catch rats or dig out a rabbit's burrow needed quickness and agility, and thus a compact body and short legs.

A dog required to haul loads needed to be strong and sturdy, and bigger to support the large masses of muscle.

Temperament was also an important factor. A large dog developed for guard duties had to have the courage to face an intruder and display aggression. An equally large dog developed to haul loads – a job in which it regularly came into contact with strangers – had to be trusting and remain calm. A small ratting dog needed to retain its innate hunting instinct so that it would immediately snap at vermin.

Top: *The ancient Egyptian dog-god Anubis, the god of the underworld.*
Left: *Dog ownership brings with it a number of therapeutic benefits, not only the joy of companionship. Dog owners suffer less stress, are less aggressive and judgmental, and live longer.*

▶ EARLY DOMESTIC DOGS ◀

The characteristics that people demanded of their dogs varied in different parts of the world, depending on the environment, climate and human lifestyle. People living in the far north needed dogs that could haul loads and withstand extremely cold weather conditions, and archaeological finds in North America show that 7500 years ago there were already dogs weighing about 23kg (50 lb) that were very similar to the Eskimo Dog of today. They had shorter muzzles than grey wolves, but almost certainly retained their ancestor's stamina and strength.

In Asia and Europe, dogs derived from Indian and Eurasian wolves were also being bred to do particular types of work, such as hunting. Greyhounds are depicted in Egyptian frescoes dated around 5000 years ago. Smaller hounds appeared that were similar to the Pharaoh Hound and Ibizan Hound we know today.

Another modern breed whose ancestors are discernible around that time is the Saluki (a tall breed; smooth coat and long fringes on the ears and tail), while a palace dog that used to be kept by the ancient Pharaohs in Egypt about 2000BC is similar to the present-day Basenji.

SIGHT HOUNDS AND SCENT HOUNDS

Most of the early dogs were hounds, which suggests that a chief objective in early dog-breeding programmes was to develop varieties suitable for hunting. The development of these varieties varied according to the part of the world in which their human owners lived.

In Egypt, animal scents quickly disseminated on the hot, dry sands. Most of the early hounds therefore relied on their vision to identify their quarry; hence the development of 'sight' or 'gaze' hounds, from which breeds such as the Afghan and Saluki were developed. These animals also needed speed (long legs and a long supple body) and stamina (a large lung capacity within a deep chest).

Animal scents lingered for much longer in the cooler and moister environments of forest and woodland – conditions common in Greece and Italy. Thick undergrowth prevented dogs from being able to follow their quarry by sight, so they needed to be able to track it by scent over long distances.

These 'scent' hounds were physically different from 'sight' hounds. They had shorter legs and more compact, muscular bodies, and were built for endurance. We know that such dogs existed several thousand years ago.

Above: *The presence of the Egyptian Pharaoh Hound spread to Europe after the Roman invasion of Egypt around 2000 years ago.*

SPITZ DOGS

These dogs have a characteristic curly tail and are represented by modern breeds such as the Siberian Husky, Samoyed and Chow Chow. There is evidence to suggest that dogs of this type were widely spread throughout the world. In China, the ancestors of the Chow Chow are featured on Han Dynasty pottery statues dated at 200BC. A northern connection came a thousand years later: the Vikings brought Spitz-type dogs (has the characterisitic appearance of a Spitz or primitive breed) with them when they invaded and settled parts of England.

OTHER EARLY DOMESTIC DOG TYPES

In China and Tibet other ancestral dog types were being developed, as pets and guard dogs, and these gave rise to short-nosed breeds such as the Pekingese, Lhasa Apso, Shih Tzu, Tibetan Spaniel, Tibetan Terrier and Japanese Chin.

In the Mediterranean region at least five or six distinctly different dog types were already in existence by Roman times. They included small dogs not unlike today's Dachshund, fast hunting dogs similar to the Greyhound, and large, heavy, guard dogs rather like the Mastiff. There were short-nosed dogs and long-nosed dogs, similar to today's Pug and Borzoi. In Britain the Celtic Hounds, forerunners of the Irish Wolfhound, were already established before the Roman invasion.

Top: *The English Springer Spaniel originated in Great Britain, and was specifically developed to pick up game birds.*

▶ THE ARRIVAL OF THE 'PET' DOG ◀

As time went by, more types of dog were developed. Dogs that could hunt by both sight and scent proved very useful as all-purpose hunters, and from them were developed the smaller 'earth' dogs, now known as terriers.

Their name comes from the word *terra*, Latin for earth. They were short-legged, tough and hardy animals, expert at detecting and catching smaller quarry and an invaluable aid in keeping down the vermin that thrived in most areas of human habitation.

Dogs required for herding cattle and sheep needed to be agile and intelligent, and these dogs needed to retain many of the characteristics of their wolf ancestors, who performed similar tasks during a hunt when singling out the weaker animals.

Larger and heavier Mastiff-type dogs were developed to pull loads, protect herds and flocks from dangerous predators such as wild bears or wolves, or guard property against both animals and humans.

The bond that exists between most of today's owners and their dogs is not new. Two thousand years ago a shepherd in Turkey probably had similar feelings about his working dog as a British, American or Australian farmer does today. But while many people would have felt the need for a dog's companionship in those early days, few could have afforded to keep and

feed a dog that did not work for its living. Pet dogs were largely the province of the wealthy. In China and Japan, 'toy' dogs were kept by the emperors and their courts, and it was only when European travellers began to visit those countries that many of the breeds were 'discovered' and brought back to Europe and England. By AD500 the Bichon family of dogs was established, giving rise to today's Bichon Frise and possibly the Lowchen. Various types of small dog were also developed in monasteries, where their role ranged from companion to watchdog.

With the passing of the centuries, more of today's breeds took shape. In AD1300 the Black Hound, forerunner of the Bloodhound, was established in Britain, while in Europe and Asia herding dogs were developing – among them the ancestors of the Hungarian Puli and the Komondor breed.

Perhaps as many as three-quarters of today's dog breeds were developed during the last 300 years or so. Improvement in the range and accuracy of firearms resulted in the introduction and refinement of many of today's gundog breeds, while increased affluence led to more interest in general purpose and toy dogs.

By the beginning of the 20th century the development was almost complete, and most of the refinements since then have been cosmetic rather than functional.

Below: *The Chow Chow, a black-tongued breed once popular in Manchuria and Mongolia, is a real one-person dog with a tendency to snap or bite at others.*

▶ DOG BREEDS AND KENNEL CLUBS ◀

Today there are hundreds of breeds (some encyclopaedias list more than 400), many of them recognized only in their country of origin. Breed standards are established, which enables breeders and judges to select progeny that come closest to the required characteristics, therefore ensuring their continuation. To gain recognition, a breed must have clearly identifiable characteristics that are passed between generations; these become the basis for the breed's establishment.

Many countries have their own Kennel Club or similar organization that controls and monitors the registration and showing of pedigree dogs. It recognizes particular breeds for show purposes and classifies them into groups based on similarities of use or characteristics.

The number of groups, their names and the breeds within them are not consistent between countries. There is some agreement about four of the groups (Toys, Gundogs/Sporting Dogs, Terriers and Hounds), but not about any others. Some countries have separate groups for work-ing dogs and herding dogs, while others have groups named non-sporting, utility or Spitz breeds (dogs with the characteristic appearance of a Spitz or primitive breed: tail curled over the back and pricked ears).

Because each country has its own method of classifying dog breeds, the Fédération Cynologique Internationale (FCI) was formed to rationalize the differences. It divides breeds into 10 groups, using its own classification system: Sheep Dogs and Cattle Dogs (other than Swiss Cattle Dogs); Pinschers and Schnauzer type, Molossian type, Swiss Mountain and Cattle dogs; large and medium-sized Terriers; Dachshunds; Spitz and primitive types; Scenthounds and related breeds; Pointing Dogs; Companion and Toy Dogs; Sighthounds; and Retrievers, Flushing Dogs and Water Dogs.

At the time of writing it had registered 331 breeds. Member countries of the FCI (78 at the time of writing) define their own breed standards but submit them to the FCI for international recognition.

Above: *The Pointer was originally bred as a hunting companion due to its excellent sight and sense of smell, coupled with its intelligence and ability to learn.*

This chapter would not be complete without a brief mention of those lovable canines of mixed or unknown ancestry. Cross-breeds are animals of known parentage from two different breeds. Mongrels are of unknown ancestry. Endowed with what scientists term hybrid vigour, they often (not always) combine some of the more desirable characteristics of their ancestors. They may not be officially recognized, but they still bring joy and comfort to millions of people.

Sadly, mongrels are the main product of uncontrolled breeding and account for the majority of unwanted puppies, or dogs 'dumped' by their owners, that end up in animal shelters. Despite endless efforts to educate owners and discourage indiscriminate breeding, this worldwide problem continues.

▶ A SPECIAL BOND ◀

These days pet animals are one of the many factors that make up what we call 'quality of life'. During the last 20 years, numerous studies have confirmed the psychological and medical benefits of pet ownership. These benefits have also become a basis for programmes based on animal-assisted activities (AAA), also referred to as 'pet-facilitated therapy' and 'animal-facilitated therapy'. In these programmes, interactions with animals are used to assist humans with physical or psychological problems.

In industrialized societies increasing affluence, a falling birth rate and looser family ties have resulted in pets playing a more important psychological role. More couples are choosing not to have any children, or to have them later in life after the female partner has established a career, and for many of these people a pet becomes an important member of the family. But regardless of your family status, owning a pet dog is likely to provide you with some very important benefits.

Inset: *Cross-breeds and mongrels account for the majority of dogs in almost every country.*
Above: *Golden Retrievers are an affection-demanding breed, and very patient towards children.*

COMPANIONSHIP

For four out of five dog owners the most important feature of owning a dog is the company it provides. Companionship may mean simply having the dog around or the dog may be a working companion or used for a specific task.

For many of us a dog acts as a safeguard against loneliness; it becomes a partner and a friend in whom we can confide. If you think you are unusual in talking to your dog as if it were another human being, don't worry. You are not.

Most of us behave in a similar way. As well as talking to our dogs, we instinctively use methods of communication that we would use with members of our own species. To console our canine companions, for example, we use standard 'primate gestures' such as stretching out our hands and patting them, pursing and smacking our lips and uttering soothing noises, although men are generally less demonstrative in this respect than women.

COMFORT

A subtle aspect of animal companionship is the physical proximity or nearness of an animal to its owner. The mere fact that our dog is in the same room as us produces a feeling of comfort, and the more attached we are to our dog the closer it may be allowed to sleep to us at night. Some dogs share their owner's bed, while others are made to sleep outside the home in their own kennel or shed.

Comfort may also come from physical contact, or from the affection it displays towards you.

RELAXATION

Your dog will help you relax. It has been conclusively demonstrated that a person in a state of tension shows a slowing of the heart rate and a drop in blood pressure when their pet comes on the scene. Owning a pet can be an important stress-management practice for people with high stress levels in their work.

PHYSICAL SECURITY AND PROTECTION

An increase in crime in some societies has resulted in more people keeping watchdogs or guard dogs as additional protection for themselves and their property. In these cases there is

Above: *The sensitive Rough Collie (right) tends to grow deeply attached to its owner. It also makes a good guard dog.*

a trend towards keeping the larger, potentially more aggressive breeds such as the Doberman, German Shepherd Dog or Rottweiler, and other breeds that have been specifically developed for guarding, such as the Neapolitan Mastiff and Dogue de Bordeaux.

But it is not just the size or potential aggressiveness of a dog that is important. For many of us, our feeling of security lies in the knowledge that the animal will detect and react to a stranger or intruder long before we can, and this gives us more time to react to such a situation. For this reason many owners of small dogs feel just as secure with their pet as they would with a large, specially trained watchdog or guard dog.

EMOTIONAL SECURITY

In addition to physical protection, a dog can also provide us with psychological protection. For example, it can give us the emotional security to face or overcome irrational fears, such as a fear of the dark or anxiety at being left alone.

If you are doing something in a strange environment, or meeting strangers, having your dog with you can enable you to carry out your tasks more effectively or communicate better. For example, one sociological study into human behaviour showed that people interviewed by a researcher accompanied by her dog generally felt more comfortable and relaxed than those interviewed without the dog present.

HELPING TO ESTABLISH NEW FRIENDSHIPS

There is plenty of evidence to show that people who like dogs are more likely to like other people, are more socially interactive, and are probably good at establishing new human friendships. Dogs certainly act as ice breakers for contact between humans. Take your dog for a walk and it is possible that a usually reserved neighbour or even a total stranger will stop and comment on its appearance or behaviour. Dogs also act as an important link between the young and the old.

SELF-FULFILMENT AND SELF-ESTEEM

We all need to feel good about ourselves. Many of us achieve this through success in our family relationships, work, sport or other recreational activities. Others achieve it through reflected glory by owning a dog that is an object of prestige. The dog may be a rare or unusual breed, a winner in the show ring or an obedience or agility champion.

For some of us the responsibility of caring for another living creature can result in a sense of self-worth, and by doing it correctly we may be rewarded by the approval of other people.

AESTHETIC SATISFACTION

Your dog doesn't have to be a show winner in order to give you pleasure. If you have chosen it for its character and appearance, then every time you look at it you will feel good.

AN AID TO LEISURE ACTIVITIES

Dogs are an important part of our leisure experience. Dogs like to play, and they stimulate us to play with them. This helps us to relax and develop a more active zest for life, diverting us from the comparative drudgery of family chores or work. For many of us merely looking after a dog, such as feeding, grooming and exercising it, can become a leisure activity in itself.

BENEFITS TO CHILDREN

About two out of three families that own a dog also have children. We might ask why parents coping with a growing family would want to adopt another, nonhuman member, and the answer is not entirely clear. Many of us think that having a pet dog will help teach our children responsibility; that a child who learns to care for a pet is more likely to have a caring attitude towards fellow humans.

There is also an educational value. If our children learn about a dog's body processes such as sexual maturity and reproduction, and how to cope with its health problems or illnesses, they may be better prepared for their own experiences later in life. The life span of a pet dog is approximately 10–15 years, and may match the period during which our children are growing to maturity. The life of our dog might help to teach them about growing up, learning, old age, suffering and death. Caring for it during that lifetime may teach them some valuable 'parenting' skills.

The presence of a pet dog in your household can help your children to overcome anxiety, control aggression, develop self-awareness and deal with life's problems.

Research has shown that children will often confide in the family dog, spending just as much time talking to it about the day's successes and failures as they do with their brothers or sisters. When their parents or siblings aren't around, the dog acts as a substitute. It is interesting to note that the children most likely to develop social skills and empathy with other people are those who talk intimately and at length with their pets and their grandparents.

EMOTIONAL SUPPORT

If your family has suffered the loss of a loved one, or a teenager is going through a particularly difficult period in his or her life, your dog can provide much-needed emotional support at such a critical time.

A RESPONSIBLE ATTITUDE, BETTER HOUSEKEEPING

Those of us who have had to put up with muddy paws through a long and wet winter may wonder how owning a dog could possibly contribute to improved hygiene, yet it has been shown that families with pets are generally more hygiene conscious than those without.

Above: *This Airedale puppy should grow up to be tough, strong and intensely faithful.*

THERAPEUTIC VALUE

Your dog will probably bring you plenty of other benefits. Statistically you are likely to:

- live longer
- have lower blood pressure
- be in less danger of heart attacks if you are prone to them
- have better motivation and be more purposeful
- be less egocentric and more supportive of others
- suffer less stress and gain more relief from tension
- be emotionally stronger and less likely to become depressed
- be less aggressive
- be less judgmental of other people faults or afflictions.

BENEFITS TO THE ELDERLY

Dogs can be of special benefit to elderly people, who often fail to feed themselves properly. Feeding their dog stimulates them to eat, too, and their dog provides them with company while they are eating.

Many elderly people are not allowed to take their dog with them when they enter a retirement home. On the other hand, there are many valid reasons why they should be allowed to have their pet with them.

▶ FAILED HUMAN-DOG RELATIONSHIPS ◀

Remember, not all dog-owner relationships are a success. Perhaps as many as one in five fail, so if your first experience in dog ownership has not been a happy one, you are not alone. Make an effort to analyze the reasons for your experience. Your vet may be able to help identify the causes.

A dog may become a problem because:

- it was wrongly selected, and doesn't fit into your environment/family/lifestyle
- it wasn't trained properly by you or allowed to socialize properly with your other pets
- there was an inherent problem in the dog's genetic make-up.

If you can identify the reasons for the problems you experienced with your previous dog, and eliminate those problems, then do try again since owning a dog can indeed add to the quality of your life.

Top: *Elderly dog owners are more motivated and purposeful than those living alone.*

A NEW DOG FOR YOU

▶ SELECTING YOUR COMPANION ◀

If you have previously owned a dog and experienced the unique bond that can develop between you, then you will know that any type of ownership involves an ongoing responsibility and long-term commitment, consideration for others and a responsible attitude towards society. You will also know that, properly treated, a dog can prove to be a loyal and affectionate friend and can give its owner many years of love and devotion.

When choosing a new dog, don't let your heart rule your head. Be aware of the size (height, length and weight) to which a puppy may grow, the amount of food it will eat, the grooming and exercise it will need, the temperament it might have, the possible health problems that might arise, and its possible life span.

Before deciding to get a dog as a pet, whether it is for the first time or as a replacement, ask yourself the following important questions:

WHAT DO YOU EXPECT FROM THE DOG?

- Do you want your pet dog to become a member of the family, sharing your home and your life?
- Do you want it to act as a watchdog to warn you when strangers arrive, or to guard your property when you are away? Most dogs, regardless of their size, will sound an alarm when something strange occurs, or if somebody appears on your premises, and in most cases they provide enough warning and protection. If you want a dog of a breed that is an ideal guard dog, it will require proper training and handling. If you don't have the expertise to do this properly, don't get one.
- Do you want it to be successful in shows or other competition, and if so, why?
- List all your expectations, then choose a breed which best suits your needs.

TO WHOM WILL IT BELONG?

Be sure you know who will be responsible for your dog and look after it. Involve all members of the family in the decision-making process, but make sure that one, committed person takes on the overall responsibility and will act as leader of the pack.

Left: *At a young age puppies have a strong need to chew, so it is important to provide them with their own toys.*

DO YOU HAVE ENOUGH KNOWLEDGE?

If you are a first-time dog owner, make sure you know what you are taking on. Your pet dog needs much more than feeding, exercise and grooming. It needs training and regular health care throughout its life, and may need special care when it is old.

DO YOU HAVE ENOUGH TIME?

You will need to devote a lot of time to bringing up and training a puppy, and to giving a juvenile and adult dog the companionship it needs. Over a period of years you will spend many thousands of hours training and generally caring for the animal.

DO YOU HAVE ENOUGH COMMITMENT?

You must be prepared to lose a certain amount of freedom, and commit for 10–15 years, perhaps longer. You may have done this once already, but are you capable of doing it again?

CAN YOU GIVE IT THE RIGHT ENVIRONMENT?

Is your home large enough for the type of dog you would like? Are there areas nearby where it can be adequately exercised? Will you be able to keep it confined to your property and prevent it from roaming around the neighbourhood?

CAN YOU AFFORD IT?

Apart from any initial cost of purchasing a dog and accessories, there are ongoing costs for food, annual vaccinations and general health care, and possibly for neutering. There may be registration fees, and costs involved in fencing your garden, attending obedience-training classes, or kennelling the dog while you are away on holiday.

CAN YOU OFFER THE DOG A STABLE HOME?

Are the circumstances of the person who is responsible for the dog likely to change in the foreseeable future? Is the owner of the dog likely to go away to university, move cities or travel overseas for any length of time? Is the proposed owner elderly or infirm, or likely to suffer health problems that might affect his or her ability to care for the dog?

WHICH SEX WILL YOU CHOOSE?

Decide if you want a male or female, and if you will consider neutering either sex. Bitches are usually smaller than males, more manageable and more easily trained. Unless they are spayed, they will have an oestrus cycle ('come into season' or 'be in heat') every six months.

IS A DOG THE RIGHT SPECIES?

Think about this very carefully. Would a cat or some other domestic pet be more suitable? It is very important to assess all your options before committing yourself.

Right: *You may be tempted to buy a puppy (or two) because of its cuteness, but remember that when it grows up, it will need more than simply feeding and exercise: it will need training, regular health care and special care when it is old.*

▸ INTEGRATING A NEW DOG WITH ONE YOU ALREADY OWN ◂

You may already own a dog, perhaps one that is getting on in years, and wish to bring another one into the household. Whether this will cause problems or not will depend on a number of factors, including the ages of the dogs and how you go about integrating them.

The two dogs will need to establish their own hierarchy within the household – which one is dominant and which subordinate. They may do this with little or no incident – a young puppy, for example, will usually defer to an older, naturally more dominant dog. There may be problems, though, if the new dog is an adolescent and decides to become the dominant dog, and your other dog objects. (For more details, see p95.)

▸ SELECTING A DOG ◂

It is important that you match your dog to your individual circumstances and your ability to look after it properly.

An old adage states that 'there are no bad dogs, merely bad owners'. In many cases it holds true, although some dogs have inherited temperamental problems. Most so-called dog problems really are owner problems, caused by a mismatch of the breed (with its needs and temperament) and the owner (with his or her temperament and lifestyle).

Such a mismatch between dog and owner can result in a dog living a socially deprived life in an entirely unsuitable environment. Under such circumstances, behavioural problems are likely to occur.

If a Terrier, whose innate instinct is to dig, is left alone in a small garden while its owners are

Top: *When you introduce your new puppy to your 'current' dog, they'll need to establish the hierarchy between them. The puppy will usually submit to the naturally dominant, older dog.*

out, it will probably wreck the flowerbeds and/or dig its way out under the fence. If a dog that craves company has to watch its owner depart for work, then spend eight hours alone, it is very likely to suffer from separation anxiety.

People wanting a dog for protection often choose a large dog of a 'guarding' breed. In many cases it is the dog's size and strength that result in it becoming a problem. If they are unwilling or unable to train it properly and control the dog when walking it on a lead, the owners often resort to leaving it to exercise itself in the garden, which is usually far too small. Feeling enclosed and frustrated, the dog becomes bored and starts to dig holes, whine, howl and bark at anything or anyone that passes by. If the garden is fenced, it will find the smallest of gaps to peer through, then bark madly the moment anyone passes by, frightening them out of their wits and giving the dog exactly the reward it needs to repeat the process. If this behaviour goes unchecked, it may become aggressive and a potential danger to visitors to its home.

PURE-BRED OR MONGREL?

There are thousands of mongrel dogs (sometimes also called cross-breeds) in dog shelters and pet shops, waiting for a loving home. Many of them will make ideal companions, and the 'hybrid vigour' that comes from their mixed (often unknown) parentage may ensure that they have a healthy constitution and are less likely to suffer from any inherited or breed-specific defects.

The main disadvantage in selecting one is that you don't know what breeds are in its parentage. You may be able to get some idea from its shape and size, but you will have far less information about its likely temperament than if you select a pure-bred animal.

If you do decide to opt for such a dog, try to insist on a trial period of at least one month to assess its behaviour.

Above: *A mongrel can make an ideal companion, although it is wise to take it home for a trial period of a month or so to discover its true temperament.*

ADOPTION

You may hear of an adult dog that needs a new home. Check the reasons for this. They may be genuine: for example, a family may be emigrating and unable to take the dog with them, or the owner may have become ill or has moved into a much smaller home, and can no longer look after the dog. On the other hand, the owner could want to part with the dog because it has behavioural problems; in this case it would be better to look elsewhere.

Some Greyhounds become available for adoption when their racing days are over. These are usually docile, make excellent companions and fit well into a family environment, but because they have been trained to chase a moving, furry object, they can be a danger to certain household or neighbourhood pets.

Individual Foxhounds and Beagles from hunting packs may also be advertised. If you decide to give a home to one of these, remember that they are very vocal and are not house-trained. In the kennel conditions under which they would have been kept, they'd have learned to urinate and defecate within the territory of their kennel compound. They have not learned substrate preference and will need immediate training to avoid accidents in the home. (For further information, see pp98–9, House soiling.) Some of these dogs never learn, so be warned. If in doubt, talk to your vet.

Above: *Retired racing Greyhounds, such as this one, make excellent companions; however, they do tend to chase anything that moves and may need careful retraining.*

SELECTING A BREED

If you already own, or have owned, a dog of a particular breed, you may decide to choose that same breed again. On the other hand, you may have owned a cross-breed or mongrel, and want to try a pure-bred dog. In that case, remember that breeds come in many different shapes, sizes and temperaments, and choosing one to suit you requires careful consideration.

Above: *If you are not sure which breed of dog is the best for your needs, talk to your vet, as he or she deals with many different dogs every day and can offer valuable advice.*

THINK ABOUT THE FOLLOWING IN RELATION TO THE BREEDS YOU ARE CONSIDERING :

- the size of dog you want as a pet

- the purpose for which you want a pet dog: companionship, show, work, obedience training or a watchdog

- your knowledge and experience of dogs; whether you have the ability to handle particular breeds

- the strength of your preferred breed, and whether you can physically handle it

- the type of home in which you live, and the amount of indoor and outdoor space

- environment in which you live: urban, semi-rural or rural

- the number and type of people who live in your home. Some breeds are not so tolerant of children; others are too boisterous with elderly or infirm people

- the amount of human companionship you can offer your dog

- the amount of time you can devote to feeding and grooming your pet

- the amount of exercise you can give the dog

- training: some breeds require firm handling and even advanced training from a professional

- your climate. Short-faced breeds (e.g. Bulldog) can suffer from breathing problems in a hot climate. For subtropical or tropical climates consider short-coated, long-nosed breeds. Breeds with long thick coats benefit from seasonal changes to assist coat shedding. Cold climate breeds include the Chow Chow, Spitz, Samoyed, Norwegian Elkhound, and Newfoundland

If you know how and why a breed was developed you are more likely to understand the nature and instinctive behaviour of the dog you hope to own.

To identify the breed that may best suit you, take the time to read about each of the breeds you fancy. Talk to your vet, because he or she deals with different breeds every day and can help you to select a suitable breed. Remember that there can be enormous variations between individuals within a particular breed, and it is essential to carefully assess every animal that you inspect before making your selection.

HOW DO YOU TELL THE DIFFERENCE BETWEEN A GOOD AND BAD BREEDER ?

- Obtain information from your national Kennel Club or breeding association.

- Get information from local dog clubs in your area.

- Talk to owners of the breed you are thinking of buying, find out if they are having any problems and where they got their animals from.

- Talk to your local veterinarian. Owners of dogs that have physical or behavioural problems as a result of poor breeding programmes usually consult vets, so these professionals get a pretty good indication of which breeders are doing the best job.

Once you have located some reputable breeders, find out why they are breeding. Some breed specifically for show, but success in the show ring does not necessarily mean that the offspring will suit you. Check out the incidence of any inherited conditions in the breeder's dogs, and if in doubt get advice about this from your vet.

CHOOSING A DOG BREEDER

Responsible breeders aim to produce healthy dogs that embody the characteristics demanded by the agreed breed standard. They also try to ensure that puppies go to owners who will properly care for them. They vet their customers and their homes before selling to them, provide clear and concise information about their breed, recommend suitable diets and advise about health care and vaccination programmes for the particular dog.

CHOOSING THE PUPPY

Never buy a puppy on the spur of the moment. Plan well ahead, allowing plenty of time for correct selection and preparation around the house for the new arrival.

If possible, visit the breeder before the bitch whelps (gives birth). Try to see both parents, and visit the puppies regularly during the suckling period. Make sure that you have a choice of puppy, rather than having a particular individual 'allocated' to you.

You may be able to obtain a puppy on a 'pet only' basis. You pay less for it, but there are conditions attached. These usually state that it cannot be registered as a pedigree dog, must not be bred from, and (more often applied to a bitch) it must be de-sexed.

Inset: *It is important that only one person becomes the official 'owner' of a dog, and takes the role of 'pack leader'.*

THE PUPPY SHOULD BE:
- aged between seven and eight weeks
- fully weaned
- strong enough to cope on its own away from its mother
- still with its mother (to enable you to assess the temperament of the bitch)
- alert, bright and healthy
- not overly aggressive towards humans or its littermates
- willing to come to you
- clean around the eyes, ears, nose and anal area, and have a healthy skin.

THE BREEDER SHOULD:
- provide the records of any de-worming or vaccinations
- provide complete information on the puppy's present and future diet
- provide pedigree papers if necessary.

YOU SHOULD:
- never obtain a puppy from a litter in which there appears to be any type of disease
- try to get the breeder to agree to a short approval period, in case there are problems
- take it on condition that it is given a thorough veterinary checkup
- have the puppy checked yourself by a vet as soon as you get it.

Top: *Only give a dog as a gift if the receiver is able to offer the stability needed by the animal.*
Above: *If you don't want your personal grooming equipment to be snatched by your puppy, don't allow it to play with its own grooming tools.*

SELECTING FOR TEMPERAMENT

You are likely to want a puppy with the ideal temperament described in the breed standards and norms. However, within any breed there are great variations between individual dogs and strains.

Selection for temperament starts with the breeder. A reputable breeder checks all the puppies for temperament and carefully monitors their progress.

Some breeders concentrate on the physical characteristics of the breed – which will win awards in the show ring – rather than good temperament. Today, however, judges at dog shows do pay more attention to temperament, and will fault any dogs that transgress.

Always buy from a reputable breeder, and check out the temperament of the puppy's mother (and father, too, where possible). This may help to eliminate any problems in the future, but the way a puppy behaves when young will not necessarily remain the same as it gets older. The most submissive puppy in a litter may become quite bold once it is away from its littermates and established in a new home, for example.

A dog's temperament can be influenced by the temperament of its owner and the environment in which it lives, too, so you and your family will have a great deal of influence on how it behaves.

Above: *The Lhasa Apso is a small, long-haired dog which is often greyish or gold, and has a well-feathered tail. It was originally bred in Tibet as an indoor watchdog, kept by Buddhist monks.*

CARING FOR YOUR DOG

▶ FROM GROOMING TO BOARDING ◀

Whether it's a puppy or a new-to-you adult, your dog's temperament, its enjoyment of life and its health are very much influenced by the way you and your family treat it.

For most people a dog represents companionship, and indeed they are great companions. However, they are not substitute human beings. They have their own needs and their own psyche. The relationship between dog and owner is a two-way street and it is important that owners understand the world from their dog's point of view. Doing so should avoid the development of some behavioural problems commonly found in canines, and will also help owners to recognize problems as they arise, to understand how to deal with these problems and where, in particular, to obtain the necessary help.

▶ A HOME FOR YOUR NEW PUPPY ◀

Between the age of three and 16 weeks a puppy goes through a particularly important learning period. During this time, new experiences will leave a lasting impression.

When it arrives at your home your new puppy will have lost the company and comfort of its mother and littermates, and will be in a strange environment. It is important that you begin the process of socialization, gently integrating your new pet into your family and teaching it to relate to people and other animals through interaction and pleasant encounters.

FREEDOM FROM STRESS

Avoid sudden loud noises, such as the slamming of doors or children's screams.

Initially, it is best to limit the number of people with whom the puppy comes into contact, gradually allowing it to get used to more and more strange faces.

Don't allow children to handle the puppy too much, or disturb it when it is resting or sleeping.

Left: *Every puppy should be provided with its own secure sleeping area, a comfortable bed and a selection of toys. If you are opting for crate training, a playpen or large travelling cage can be used in this designated area.*

COMFORT

Provide a warm, comfortable bed. If you can't afford a proper dog bed or basket, use a large cardboard box with the sides cut down slightly. Line the bottom with a thick layer of newspaper and top this with a washable blanket. If you decide to buy a proper dog bed or basket, make sure it is large enough to accommodate your puppy as it grows.

Place the puppy's bed where you want it to sleep as an adult – choose a quiet, private corner. For the first few nights a big cuddly toy and a warm (not hot) water bottle beneath the bedding will help the puppy settle. It may be noisy and distressed immediately after separation from its littermates. A low radio or ticking clock can help soothe it. During its waking hours, give the puppy plenty of body contact.

Talk to it, using a soft voice to express friendship and a gruff voice to express disapproval of any unwanted actions.

SAFETY PRECAUTIONS

When preparing for your new puppy's arrival, consider safety in the home, just as you would in the case of a young child.

• Lock away all household chemicals or any poisons, and remove garden toxins such as snail bait.

• Keep electrical cords out of biting reach.
• Don't leave food wrapped in plastic, foil or paper packaging where your puppy can reach it.
• Make sure your puppy can't get into rubbish bins; it could suffocate.
• Be aware of the risks associated with some common house and garden plants.
• Remember that sparks from an open fire or hot cigarette ash can damage your puppy's eyes or skin.
• Anyone using mowers, bicycles, skateboards, Roller Blades and other similar articles must be extra vigilant.
• Check where the puppy is before moving a car.
• Make sure that your puppy cannot get through fencing around a swimming pool.

Top: *This teething Dogue de Bordeaux finds some relief in his squeaky toy.*
Above: *A selection of safe, chewable dog toys.*

INFECTIONS YOU COULD CATCH FROM YOUR DOG

Some dog infections can be passed on to humans: rabies; intestinal parasites such as roundworms, hookworms and tapeworms; leptospirosis and other bacterial infections such as campylobacter and salmonella; and ringworm infection.

- Avoid contamination from a dog's urine or faeces.
- Wash your hands after handling a dog.
- Don't allow a dog to lick your face.
- Don't eat food that may have been licked by a dog.

HOUSE RULES

Your puppy is a member of your family 'pack', which includes humans and other family pets. You must teach it some house rules: that you are the pack leader, and that it is the bottom dog in the pack. Once your puppy recognizes its place in your family hierarchy it will be more contented and more easily trained to obey commands.

You will need to start teaching your new puppy house rules. Then, once it has settled in, you can start to teach it the basic commands (see pp74–6, Training you dog).

FOOD AND WATER

First find out what your puppy was eating before it joined your family, then start off by feeding the dog the same diet. Introduce any changes over several days to avoid causing digestive upsets. Specially formulated and fully balanced commercial puppy diets are strongly recommended. Make sure that clean, fresh water is always available. A deep, stainless-steel or earthenware bowl will keep the water cooler, and in summer ice can be added.

PLAY, TOYS AND CHEWING

Puppies thrive on play. Among their own littermates it gives them exercise and it is how they learn to compete for their order in the pack. Don't be rough with your puppy, but in these early games it is important that the dog learns that the family members are dominant; express disapproval if it tries to get the upper hand.

Puppies chew objects partly because it helps them through the teething process and partly because it is a way of investigating their environment. Satisfy this need with chewable toys or objects, but make sure these are:
- made of safe materials
- large enough so that they cannot be swallowed
- dissimilar to objects you don't want chewed. For example, if you provide your puppy with an old slipper to chew, don't be surprised if it decides to cut its teeth on one of your expensive shoes. It will be too young to have learned the difference. Rawhide chews are ideal, because your puppy cannot mistake them for anything else.

HOUSE-TRAINING

Training should begin as soon as the puppy arrives in its new home. Puppies learn very quickly at a young age. An eight-week-old puppy can learn quite a few of the basic commands within a seven-day period. Reinforce reward-based training – your puppy receives a food treat each time it performs a particular desirable behaviour – as they are very food-orientated at this stage.

It is best to adopt your puppy when it is seven or eight weeks old, as it is around this time that it is beginning to develop what is known as a 'substrate preference': the selection of a specific substance and area on which to eliminate. This means that it will quickly become accustomed to using grass or soil as a toilet area if given ready access and encouraged to do so.

Anticipate toilet needs. Take your puppy outside as soon as it wakes up, as well as before and after every meal, after a period of vigorous play or exercise and whenever you see it looking distracted, walking in circles and sniffing the ground. It is important to go right outside with the puppy, take it to a specific area of the garden and wait until it has eliminated. Always praise it afterwards. Never stand at the door and wait for the puppy to take itself outside. The chances are it will wander off a little way and then come straight back to find you – without relieving itself.

If you wish, you can use a word command (many trainers use the word 'busy') when you take the puppy outside. It will soon learn to associate the word with the action. Once that is taught, you can train it to eliminate at home rather than in a public place. Always clean up the faeces (a poop-scoop is ideal) and dispose of them properly.

Never allow a young puppy free access to the entire house. It can become disoriented and relieve itself in one of the rooms. You need to be there to take it outside if it needs to go.

Young puppies have small bladders and poor bladder control. Don't expect a young puppy to manage without urinating from 20:00 to 8:00. Take it out late at night – 23:00 is a good time, and get up at 5:00 to let it out once more.

If your puppy eliminates in the house, do not become angry and punish it. If you have not seen the puppy make the mistake, just clean it up and forget about it. If you catch the puppy in the act, say 'no' firmly. Then pick up the puppy, take it outside and praise it while it is on the grass. If possible, take the 'mistake' out with you on a paper towel so that the puppy associates the waste product with the outdoor surface.

Because a puppy has an attention span of only a few seconds, you cannot demonstrate that something is wrong some time after it was done.

Above: *Remember that if you house-train a puppy on newspaper, this will become its 'substrate preference', and it could relieve itself on your weekend papers.*

▶ SOCIALIZATION ◀

Your puppy will need to learn to socialize with any other animals in your household.

If you own a cat, ask your vet to trim its claws to avoid it damaging the puppy's eyes. Do not allow the puppy to chase the cat, and if necessary keep it on a lead when the cat is around. Distract it whenever it wants to chase the cat and gradually encourage closer contact in a controlled manner.

If you own another dog, introduce the dog and puppy outside the house. Give the older dog plenty of attention and supervise all play. Feed the dogs separately, and don't leave them alone together until the puppy is well settled in. Even then, it is wise to provide the puppy with an area into which it can escape from the other dog. Try a wooden box or a kennel with a door too small for the larger dog.

Don't allow your puppy to meet with neighbourhood dogs until it has completed its vaccination programme. If possible enrol the puppy in a puppy preschool (see p73, Training your dog).

If you own other types of animals, introduce these to the puppy early on. Allow the puppy to be present when you are attending to them, and encourage the puppy to behave gently.

Allow the puppy to meet human visitors, but make sure that such meetings are carried out gently and quietly so that the puppy enjoys the experience. Prevent children who visit from handling the puppy roughly.

Top: *Although a dog and cat living in the same household may become tolerant of and affectionate with each other, felines are too independent to act as day-care companions for a dog.*

Confine your puppy to a small area of your home until it is properly toilet-trained. A mobile playpen can prove very successful indoors, and can also be used to allow the puppy some time outside in the garden.

Once it is toilet-trained, your puppy can be given as much freedom around the house as you choose.

Make sure that your garden is properly fenced and that gates have return springs and catches on them. Because dogs are naturally territorial, it won't be long before your puppy learns to recognize the boundaries of its own property.

You must limit contact with other dogs until it has completed a course of vaccinations, usually at the age of 12 or 16 weeks. You can attend a reputable puppy preschool (preferably run in association with a veterinary clinic) before the puppy's vaccination programme is complete, because these schools should be held in a disease-free environment (see p73, Training your dog).

Avoid parks, forests and other public places where other dog owners walk their pets.

If local laws permit, it is safe to take your puppy for early morning walks on the beach below the high-tide mark – the sand will have been washed overnight by the high tide and is unlikely to have been contaminated since.

Do not go onto the dry sand and you will need to clean up after your puppy for the sake of other walkers.

- **Vaccinations**
  See p106, Protecting your dog's health.

- **Worming**
  See pp111–6, Protecting your dog's health.

- **Flea control**
  See pp118–20, Protecting your dog's health.

- **Lead training and exercise**
  Once it is fully vaccinated, your puppy will benefit from regular exercise, and by then you will need to have trained it to wear a collar and walk on a lead.

- **Collar and leash training**
  See pp79–81, Training your dog.

Above: *It is essential that your puppy has a quiet, private corner in which to sleep.*

▶ EXERCISING YOUR PUPPY ◀

Exercise your puppy only to a degree that it can comfortably manage. Don't force it, and don't attach it to a bike or person in such a way that it has to exercise regardless of how it feels. A retractable lead is ideal, as it gives the puppy a chance to pace itself. Stop exercise immediately if it begins to look tired or stressed.

If you want to run with your puppy, limit this activity to very short spells. Be very careful with a puppy of a large breed, because its bone growth is much slower than average and excessive exercise can cause ligament or bone damage. If in doubt, don't run with it, and talk to your vet or breeder.

Before going out, use your chosen word command to try to get it to eliminate at home (see p38, House-training). If this is not successful and the dog eliminates while you are out, make sure you pick up the droppings and dispose of them properly – many local authorities now provide dog waste bins. Dog faeces containing certain roundworm or hookworm eggs or larvae can be a hazard to human health (see also pp111–6, Protecting your dog's health).

▶ TEETHING AND DENTAL HYGIENE ◀

Between the ages of three and six months your puppy's temporary (milk) teeth will gradually be shed and replaced by permanent teeth.

You can help your puppy through this teething process by providing soft foods, although rawhide chews are also ideal for young puppies as the chewing action helps to loosen the temporary teeth, and is beneficial for tartar control. A proper diet will help to keep teeth clean and gums healthy. A dog toothpaste, for tartar control, is also available from vets. Train your puppy so that it will allow you to apply this with a soft toothbrush. Special diets are available that will clean teeth through their mildly abrasive action.

Top: *Regular interactive play reinforces the bond between you and your dogs.*

▶ GROOMING YOUR DOG ◀

BRUSHING AND COMBING

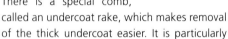

As soon as you get your puppy you should get it used to being groomed, handled and examined. Establish a daily routine in which the puppy is gently placed onto a nonslip surface (a piece of old carpet or something similar), either on the floor or on a table, and rolled over to have its mouth, teeth, eyes, ears, abdomen, paws and other parts of its anatomy examined. Although it may not need grooming, do it anyway. This routine will train your puppy to accept being handled and groomed, and you will more quickly detect fleas or flea dirt, and any hair or skin problems.

Try to make each session pleasant for the puppy, and praise and reward it for good behaviour.

Your basic grooming equipment should include a dog brush, comb, grooming glove (mitt), a sponge, cotton wool balls, dog towel, blunt-ended surgical scissors and nail clippers.

Dog brushes are especially designed for different types of coat. Those with soft bristles will avoid damage to the sensitive skin of fine-coated breeds.

Brushes with hard bristles can be used on thick-coated breeds, while rubber brushes are suitable for use on breeds with very short, close coats (e.g. Boxers), and soft, pin brushes are ideal for breeds with long, fine coats such as the Yorkshire Terrier.

Combs also vary. Those with wide teeth are used on long, fine coats, while those with narrow teeth are suitable for other types of coat and can be used to remove tangles from the ears, leg feathers or tail. There is a special comb, called an undercoat rake, which makes removal of the thick undercoat easier. It is particularly useful for Labrador Retrievers and German Shepherd Dogs (Alsatians).

You will spend more time grooming a long-coated breed than a short-coated one. Pay special attention to the feathering on the legs, and the tail. Also check the paws, nails and paw pads. Use a wet sponge to wash away any mud that has accumulated on the hair between the pads, to prevent it building up and causing inflammation. As your puppy gets bigger, hair may grow beyond the level of the pads. If so, trim it away using a pair of blunt-ended, curved surgical scissors.

Use a damp cotton wool ball to wipe away 'sleep' from your dog's eyes. Check under the tail, wipe away any debris and cut away any excess hair that might lead to soiling.

This page: *A hard bristle brush is ideal for thick-coated dogs. It is also useful to acquire a double-sided comb, an undercoat rake, and a grooming mitt for proper coat care.*

BATHING

If you carry out regular grooming, you should need to bath your dog only if it gets very dirty or smelly.

Always give your dog a thorough brush-out before bathing it. Use lukewarm water (which is more comfortable, especially for a puppy) and a proper dog shampoo. Place a cotton wool ball in each ear to prevent water from entering, and don't let shampoo get into any body opening. Rinse off thoroughly, paying special attention to the areas between the forelegs and hind legs.

A puppy can easily become chilled, so make sure you dry it properly, using its own special towel. If you prefer to use a hair dryer, run your fingers through the dog's hair as it is being dried to make sure that the air stream is not too hot for its sensitive skin.

NAILS

Dogs' nails, like those of humans, are continually growing. Puppies need their nails clipped about every six weeks, with special dog nail clippers. It is possible to do them yourself, but perhaps rather ask a vet or dog groomer.

Many adult dogs spend little time walking on hard surfaces, so their nails don't wear down naturally. Nail growth and wear varies according to breed and conditions, so clip your dog's nails as necessary.

If your puppy has dewclaws (an additional claw that serves no function), regularly check their length. Unless properly trimmed, the claws may catch in objects and get torn. In extreme cases the nails may eventually curl round and grow back into the skin.

DOG GROOMERS AND GROOMING PARLOURS

Many breeds require a considerable amount of grooming. Other breeds require clipping if their owner wants them to conform to the breed's usual appearance or enter them into shows. If you are sure that you know exactly what to do, and if you have the time, you can do all this grooming yourself. If not, get a professional to do it for you. If you would like to learn to groom your dog, ask at your nearest grooming parlour or veterinarian for details of grooming schools and courses. It would be wise to ease your dog into the grooming process, as most dogs will not stay still while being handled, especially when giving them a bath (generally, dogs do not like water).

Above: *As most dogs spend their time on soft outdoor terrain or carpets, their nails don't wear down naturally. You'll need to clip their nails regularly – if you're unsure, ask your vet to do so.*

▶ DE-SEXING ◀

Unless your dog is to be used for pedigree breeding, it is important to have it de-sexed (spayed or neutered). The recommended ages for de-sexing are five to six months for females, before their first oestrus period, and six months or more for males. Ask your vet for advice. De-sexing has many advantages, above the obvious one of avoiding an unwanted pregnancy and adding to the number of puppies in need of a good home. This procedure helps avoid various forms of cancer in the dog or bitch (such as prostate and mammary cancer), as well as reduces a male dog's sex drive (and therefore its levels of frustration).

▶ DAY CARE ◀

If you regularly have to leave your dog on its own for more than four hours at a stretch, consider employing a dog walker or dog sitter. A full, eight-hour working day is too long to regularly leave it alone; dogs left for such long periods are more likely to develop bad habits or anti-social behaviour. And, while another dog may provide company, cat companionship is unlikely to be enough for a dog – although it would help.

▶ TRAVELLING WITH YOUR DOG ◀

THE LAW

Whenever you take your dog away from home, put your name and telephone number on a dog tag and fasten this to its collar. If your dog gets lost, you have a better chance of being re-united with it. Make sure you know the laws that apply to the locality to which you are travelling. In many areas local laws require dogs to be walked on a lead. Dogs may be prohibited altogether in parks and on beaches, or restricted to certain seasons or times of day. In most places you are expected to clean up after your dog and remove the waste.

IN YOUR CAR

If possible, train your dog from puppyhood so that it becomes used to travelling. This will help eliminate any fear or agitation, and reduce the likelihood of motion sickness.

Do not allow your dog to have complete freedom within a vehicle. It can distract the driver and lead to an accident, and the dog is at risk of injury if an accident occurs. For its own safety a dog should ride in the rear of a station wagon or hatchback. Fit a special grill or dog guard to prevent it from jumping onto the seats in front.

If your dog has to travel on the back seat, fasten it into a seat belt. If it is small enough, train it to ride comfortably in a plastic travelling container (crate) that is fastened to a seat belt or placed in such a way that it will not move if you brake suddenly.

If there is room to put a dog crate in your vehicle, train your dog to ride in one. It even-

tually becomes an extension of its home territory, and your dog will feel comfortable inside and readily occupy it. Crates are commonly used by people who show their dogs, and are an ideal way of providing a safe, secure, 'personal space' for your canine companion. Once your dog is accustomed to it, the crate can become a 'home from home'.

If you have to leave your dog in your car, do so only briefly, make sure that the vehicle is parked in the shade and has adequate ventilation. In the sun, the temperature inside a closed car can exceed 40°C (104°F), and heatstroke will set in very rapidly. Do not assume that a car parked in the shade will remain so: as the sun moves around, a shady area may become fully exposed.

Special screens can be fixed to open windows to prevent the dog from escaping but provide enough ventilation for it.

ON HOLIDAY

Make sure that your dog's vaccinations are up to date, as the incidence of infectious disease in your holiday area may be greater than in your home neighbourhood. Different sorts of external parasite, such as ticks, may also be present, so thoroughly groom your dog every day and check its skin for their presence. Make a note of veterinary clinics in the area.

Top: *Your dog is unlikely to enjoy travelling in a cage; nevertheless, you can make the experience less traumatic by gradually introducing your dog to the idea ahead of time.*

IN A BUS, TRAIN OR PLANE

If you are taking some form of commercial transport, your dog may be required to travel separately in a crate. This can be a frightening experience for a dog that has not been crate-trained, so take the time to teach your dog to feel safe in its own crate, with its own familiar toys and bedding. And don't feed your dog six hours before the start of the journey. If you think your dog may suffer from motion sickness, ask your veterinarian for advice.

TRAVELLING BETWEEN COUNTRIES

Travel between countries usually involves travel documentation for you and your dog. Regulations vary, so make sure you know what they are for the particular country you are heading for. You will probably need a veterinary certificate stating that your dog is fit to travel and is free from any infectious or contagious disease. You will also need an up-to-date rabies vaccination certificate. Many countries require the relevant documents to be in their own language.

There are many countries where rabies does not exist. Some countries require a dog to be quarantined upon entry, while others will allow entry providing that certain conditions, such as microchip identification and blood testing, have been met (see PETS p47). Contact the consulate or embassy of the country concerned.

If travelling abroad requires you and your dog to be separated, carry out the training procedures recommended for commercial travel on a bus, train or plane.

Top: *If you plan to take your dog with you when you emigrate, bear in mind that it may have to be kept in quarantine for up to six months in certain countries.*

PET TRAVEL SCHEME (PETS)

A pilot scheme for the issue of 'pet passports' was introduced in Britain in 2000. Under this scheme, dogs and cats are allowed to travel from the British Isles to specified countries in western Europe without having to endure six months of quarantine upon their return. Dog owners must use designated carriers and ports of entry. Under the same scheme dogs and cats resident in the specified European countries are allowed to enter the British Isles.

DOGS RESIDENT IN THE BRITISH ISLES

To qualify for a 'pet passport' a dog resident in the British Isles must have an identification microchip inserted under the skin, and then be vaccinated against rabies by an approved vet. After about 30 days a blood sample is sent to a government-approved laboratory; if it passes the test, a health certificate or passport is issued.

Between 24 and 48 hours before returning to Britain, the animal must be treated against a particular tapeworm (*Echinococcus multilocularis*) and ticks, and a certificate must be issued by a vet approved by the relevant government. Once a dog has been vaccinated against rabies, booster vaccinations are required every year.

DOGS RESIDENT IN EUROPE

Animals resident in specified countries in Europe can also qualify to enter Britain. However, their owners must wait for six months from the time a successful blood test sample was taken.

DOGS RESIDENT IN THE UNITED STATES AND CANADA

Because rabies is endemic in North America, the original PET Travel Scheme did not apply to dogs entering from that region. At present, these dogs must still endure a six-month quarantine period in Britain, although the situation will be reviewed once the success of the initial scheme has been assessed.

▸ BOARDING ◂

Early training at being parted from you can help your dog to cope. You could leave it with a relative, friend or neighbour for short periods to get it used to being separated, and to learn that you will be coming back.

The standard of boarding kennels varies. Usually the more expensive the fees the better the quality of service you should expect.

A reputable kennel will allow you to inspect its facilities beforehand. If you do so, observe how the resident dogs are behaving and talk to the staff about feeding, grooming and exercise routines. The staff at your local veterinary clinic may be able to recommend a suitable boarding kennel, and will advise on vaccination procedures.

DOG SITTERS

If you don't like the idea of boarding your dog, you may wish to employ the services of a dog sitter or house minder to provide live-in care for your home and dog during your absence. Check with your vet to find out which ones are approved in your locality.

NUTRITION

▸ A BALANCED DIET ◂

The wolf and other wild members of the dog family *(Canidae)* are carnivores and eat a great deal of animal protein. But because a diet of meat alone does not contain many essential nutrients, they consume a variety of vegetable matter, either directly or in the stomach contents of their prey, as well as other types of food, including insects.

▸ NUTRIENTS AND A BALANCED DIET ◂

Dogs, like wolves, cannot remain healthy on a diet of meat alone. They also need fat, carbo-hydrates, minerals, vitamins and fibre. (If you wish to incorporate large amounts of vegetable protein in your dog's diet, consult your veterinarian.)

ENERGY

Dogs must be fed enough calories (kilojoules) to satisfy their energy needs, which vary according to their age, size and the amount of exercise or work they perform. The amount of energy that a dog requires is also related to the surface area of its body, because this influences how much heat it loses. On a kilo-per-kilo (or pound-per-pound) basis, a small dog has a comparatively larger surface area than a large dog. A dog weighing 2.5kg (5.5 lb) has 300 per cent more surface area per kilogram of body weight than a dog weighing 50kg (110 lb), so the smaller one needs more energy, kilo per kilo (or pound per pound.) The only way to determine the exact amount of energy your dog needs is to monitor its weight and health on a continuous basis. Probably about one-third of all family dogs exceed their ideal weight – and overweight dogs, just like over-weight humans, are more likely to develop health problems.

When very high intakes of energy or nutrients are needed, such as when a dog is performing hard work (Greyhound racing, sled dog) or a bitch during the late stages of pregnancy or lactation, they must be in sufficiently concen-trated form to enable the dog to physically eat the quantity of food required.

Properly formulated commercial diets will ensure your dog gets the necessary nutrients and energy it requires to maintain good health at the different stages of its development.

Left: *It is essential to feed your dog a nutritious and well-balanced diet in order to maintain a healthy coat, and strong bones and teeth.*

COMPARATIVE ENERGY REQUIREMENTS

100% Sedentary
400% Bitch during late pregnancy/lactation
300% Very hard work
200% Moderate work
170% Very cold weather
150% Slight stress (e.g. showing or training)

Giant breeds could need up to 50% more energy than shown in the table, and there may be a variation of 20% either way, depending on the dog.

▶ DIETS FOR DIFFERENT SITUATIONS ◀

Dogs need different types of diet according to:
- age or stage of growth – puppy, juvenile, adult or elderly
- the amount of exercise/work they perform
- whether a bitch is pregnant or lactating
- breed (large breeds mature later than small breeds, and giant breeds have special needs)
- size (there can be significant differences in size within a breed)
- their state of health.

SUGGESTED LEVELS OF NUTRIENTS FOR DOGS

Note: These figures are expressed as a percentage of dry matter in the diet.

	Protein	Suggested Range	Fat	Carbohydrate
Growth	32	28–32	15	40
Adult maintenance	22	22–25	8	50
Adult hard work	34	30–36	20	34
Adult very hard work	38	36–45	25	25
Pregnancy/lactation	32	25–32	15	40
Old age	22	15–22	8	50

Recommendations vary, and these figures are given as a guide only. If you want to formulate a home-cooked diet for your dog, you should discuss it with your veterinarian.

▶ COMMERCIAL OR HOME-COOKED FOODS ◀

If you choose home-cooked foods, you need to think about the considerable time involved in preparation. Will you always be able to manage to keep up with a home-cooked diet? And can you accurately provide all the nutritional requirements for your dog? You may also need to consider value for money. Most owners base their dog's diet on commercial foods, but may feed them a home-cooked meal sometimes. It doesn't hurt to ring the changes.

If you own a young puppy or a pregnant bitch, it is probably more sensible to choose a commercial diet, designed to provide all the nutritional requirements for growth and development. Of particular concern are calcium and phosphorus levels and their ratio (they should be equal) – it is difficult to get the balance right in a home kitchen. Geriatric dogs also need special care, and commercial diets are available to cater for their changing needs.

Below: *It is usually best to feed a young puppy a high-quality commercial diet, which has been formulated to accurately provide all the nutritional requirements.*

▶ COMMERCIAL DIETS ◀

Reputable commercial foods are based on sound research into the requirements of animals at each stage of development. Many commercial companies employ nutritional scientists and veterinarians to analyze their products and carry out controlled feeding trials to ensure that they meet international standards. The fully balanced commercial diets are easy to feed, and quantities can be accurately measured.

Commercial diets can be grouped according to moisture content (there is some variation between similar products):

- Canned or moist foods. These have a moisture content of around 78 per cent. They do not need preservatives because cooking destroys all bacteria and the canning prevents any further contamination.
- Dog sausages or dog rolls. These have a moisture content of around 50 per cent. They usually contain preservatives, but also require refrigeration.
- Semi-moist foods. These have a moisture content of around 25 per cent. These foods usually contain preservatives and do not require refrigeration. They often have a high carbohydrate or sugar content, so they should not be fed to diabetic dogs.
- Dry foods (complete diets). These have a moisture content of around 10 per cent, usually contain preservatives and do not require refrigeration. They are easily stored, hygienic and available for all breeds and ages of dog. (There are brands free of preservatives.)
- Biscuits. These have a moisture content of around eight per cent. They usually contain preservatives and do not require refrigeration.

Nutritionally, there is no difference between dry foods and moist foods, as long as they contain the same amount and proportion of nutrients. In general, though, moist dog foods are more costly to the consumer because they contain water, which provides no nutrition and for which the customer pays.

There are few warning signs for an inferior product, except that the label may give little or no nutritional information.

The label usually lists the main food ingredients, an analysis of certain nutrients (protein, salt and fat) and the fibre content. Many manufacturers state the amount that should be fed relative to body weight, stage of growth and activity level. They also list the calorific value of the food (in KCal/kJ per kilogram or ounce), which may help you to determine the right amount to feed your particular dog.

DOG TREATS AND DOG CHEWS

These usually contain high levels of fat and carbohydrate. Offer them to your dog when it needs something to keep it interested, or as a reward. Do make allowances for their high energy content, though, and reduce your dog's normal food intake accordingly.

Top and right: *There is no nutritional difference between moist foods and dry foods (above and right), although moist foods are usually more expensive.*

FOODS FROM THE VETERINARY CLINIC

Some commercial dog foods are sold through veterinary clinics and/or pet stores only. Referred to as professional formulae, they differ from supermarket foods in that their constituents are guaranteed. They do not contain the textured vegetable protein (TVP) found in some supermarket pet foods.

Other foods sold only through veterinary clinics are therapeutic diets formulated to assist in the management of health problems. Special diets are available for pregnant or lactating bitches, to assist dogs convalescing after surgery or trauma, or for those undergoing treatment for anaemia or cancer.

Diets are available to help with oral hygiene, and biscuits to help reduce plaque build-up.

▶ HOME-COOKED DIETS ◀

If you intend to feed your dog mainly a home-cooked diet, make sure that the mixture of foods will supply the right types and quantities of nutrients.

WARNING

Excessive supplementation with vitamins and minerals can cause serious health problems.

A popular type of home-cooked meal is lean mince or cheap meat cuts cooked together in a pressure cooker with a mixture of vegetables and perhaps pasta or rice. You can prepare this meal in bulk and freeze dinner-size packs. A commercial dog biscuit may be fed for breakfast, and the main meat meal fed at night.

Cooking food destroys some vitamins, and overcooking can greatly reduce a food's nutritional value. You would therefore need to supplement cooked foods with the right types and amounts of vitamins, just as reputable pet food manufacturers do.

Supplements usually contain calcium carbonate or bone meal (to create the right balance of phosphorus and calcium), iodine, vitamin A and vitamin D. Properly formulated supplements and herbal preparations are available from pet stores and/or veterinary clinics. It is best, though that you talk to your veterinarian before using any.

Supplementation may be necessary under certain conditions, such as stress or illness – ask your veterinarian for advice; special therapeutic diets are also available.

Top: *The ingredients for a home-made maintenance diet: make sure that the mixture provides the correct types and quantities of nutrients.*

▸ A HOME-MADE MAINTENANCE DIET ◂

This diet is for maintenance only – when a dog is already in good health and not under any stress. It is formulated to balance the nutritional deficiencies in meat. Liver provides vitamins A, D and E and various B vitamins. Corn oil provides essential fatty acids, while bone meal provides calcium and phosphorus in the correct proportions. Iodized salt provides iodine.

This quantity is for a 10kg (22 lb) dog, and should be adjusted for dogs that are lighter or heavier. The serving size will depend on the calorie requirements of the dog – the total energy value of this quantity formula is 750 KCal (3140kJ). This formula will keep in the refrigerator for a few days. However, like us, dogs enjoy freshly cooked food, which tastes better than 'cold warmed-up' meals.

Rice, brown or white (dry)	140g (5oz)
Meat (medium fat)	70g (2.5oz)
Liver	30g (1oz)
Bone meal	8g (.3oz)
Iodized salt	3g (.1oz)
Corn oil	5ml (one teaspoon)
Water	420ml (14 fl oz)

Mix the rice and water and simmer for about 20 minutes. Add the other ingredients and simmer for a further 10 minutes.

A meatier, more tasty diet can be prepared by transposing the quantities of rice and meat. The energy value will be the same, but the diet will contain almost twice the protein.

INGREDIENTS FOR HOME-COOKED MEALS

Even if you intend to serve only commercially prepared foods to your dog, don't skip this useful section about serving those little extras such as eggs, milk and oils.

MEAT AND MEAT BY-PRODUCTS

All forms of red or white meat provide protein, B-group vitamins, fat and energy, but the relative amounts depend on the type of meat and also on the cut.

All meat and offal are seriously deficient in calcium and slightly deficient in phosphorus, and the proportion of phosphorus to calcium is greatly excessive, ranging from about 10:1 for rabbit and ox heart to 30:1 for veal and 360:1 for fresh liver. Dogs need a 1:1.3 phosphorus to calcium ratio.

Meat is also deficient in vitamins A and D and iodine, copper, iron, magnesium and sodium. Meat is most nutritious if raw, but, depending on its source, you may have to cook it. In an effort to eliminate the hydatid tapeworm (see p115), certain countries require that all sheep or goat meat (or raw offal) must

	Protein (average %)	Fat (average %)	Energy (KCal/100g/3.5 c
Beef	20	4.5	122
Chicken	20	4.5	122
Lam	20	8.8	162

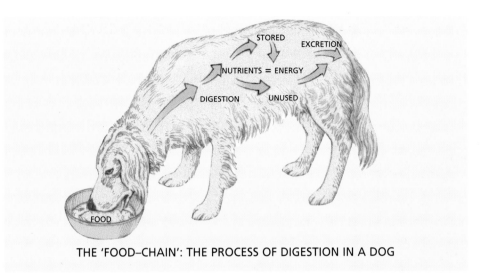

THE 'FOOD–CHAIN': THE PROCESS OF DIGESTION IN A DOG

either be cooked to a certain temperature or deep frozen at a given temperature for a minimum period of time.

The cooking process destroys much of meat's vitamin B content.

Liver is a valuable food rich in protein, fat, the fat-soluble vitamins A, D and E and the B vitamins. Too much vitamin A can lead to abnormal bone growth, but cooking reduces the liver's vitamin A content. As a general guide, do not let liver form more than 15 per cent of your dog's diet.

Chicken is considered to be more digestible than red meat, while some dogs are allergic to certain proteins contained in red meat and may develop a skin irritation.

FISH

There are two main types of fish: white, which has a nutrient composition similar to that of lean meat; and fatty or oily, which contains high levels of vitamins A and D. All fish contains high-quality protein and iodine, but is deficient in calcium, phosphorus, copper, iron, magnesium and sodium.

Take care not to feed your dog too much raw (filleted) fish, as it contains thiaminase, an enzyme that destroys thiamine, one of the B vitamins. Never give fish heads or fish offal. Cook any fish you feed. Oily fish (such as tuna) contains high levels of unsaturated fatty acids, and too much may cause a painful inflammation of fat deposits under the skin (steatitis).

Fish bones should be fed only if previously softened by pressure cooking or grinding them in a blender. Boiling or stewing would also soften the bones, but the longer cooking time would destroy more of the nutrients.

Whole fish cooked in a pressure cooker is nutritionally better than meat, as it has a better balance of nutrients.

This page and opposite: *Fish, and meat and meat by-products provide high nutritional value and variation to your dog's diet.*

EGGS

Eggs contain iron, protein, most vitamins (except for vitamin C) and carbohydrates, and are particularly good if fed raw. However, too much raw egg may be harmful, as egg white contains a substance called avidin that can reduce the availability of the B vitamin biotin (essential for many body processes, including health of skin and hair and proper muscle function). As a guide, feed no more than two raw eggs per week to a 30kg (66 lb) dog. If you feed the egg yolk only, you may increase the number of eggs to four. Hard boiling reduces the avidin, although this slightly reduces the nutritional value of the eggs.

MILK AND CHEESE

Dairy produce is high in protein, fat, carbohydrate, calcium, phosphorus, and vitamin A and the B vitamins.

Milk is a useful source of calcium for puppies, although not all dogs will drink it. It contains milk sugar (lactose), and as puppies mature their ability to digest this decreases – if fed more than small quantities of milk they may develop diarrhoea. Some adult dogs are lactose intolerant, and if fed milk they will develop an allergic, dry, itchy skin condition. Cheese is a useful source of animal protein, and most dogs like it. Serve it in chunks. It contains little or no lactose, so it can be fed to dogs that are known to have an intolerance. You can also feed unpasteurized yoghurt to dogs that are lactose intolerant.

FATS AND OILS

Fat acts as a carrier for fat-soluble vitamins (A, D, E and K), and contains substances called fatty acids (one of which is linoleic acid) which promote a healthy skin and coat; a deficiency produces an itchy skin that may become dry and scaly.

Fat is almost 100 per cent digestible and adds palatability to food. Vegetable oils and fish fats are nutritionally better than animal fats. If the diet is not already balanced, you can feed very small amounts of cod liver oil (20 small drops per 10kg/22 lb of bodyweight, per day). Excessive amounts may cause a painful inflammation of fat under the skin, called steatitis.

Never feed your dog used cooking oil, for it may contain toxic substances called peroxides.

VEGETABLES

Dogs, like cats, can synthesize vitamin C in their body and don't require a dietary source.

Vegetables are a good source of B-group vitamins, but overcooking will destroy these. So, just as with cooking for humans, it is best

This page and opposite: *Even if you serve your dog a commercially prepared diet, eggs, cheese, fish, fats and vegetables can offer highly nutritious variations.*

to lightly cook in a little water. The cooking water can be added to the meal as well. Root vegetables are a good source of vitamin A, and should be cooked to increase digestibility.

Peas and beans provide protein, energy and B vitamins, and soya beans are a particularly rich source of protein and energy.

One drawback to feeding your animal peas and beans is their tendency to form gas during digestion and cause flatulence. Flatulence can also result from feeding a multitude of other foods: high levels of milk or milk products, high protein diets, potatoes, cauliflower, cabbage and onions, to name but a few!

GRAINS
Grains provide carbohydrate, and some proteins, minerals and vitamins. They are generally deficient in fat, essential fatty acids and the fat-soluble vitamins A, D and E. Wheatgerm contains thiamine and vitamin E.

YEAST
Rich in B vitamins as well as some essential minerals, yeast preparations are good for older dogs and are safe, even when administered in excess.

FIBRE
Your dog's normal diet should contain approximately five per cent fibre (measured on a dry basis), derived from vegetable matter. Fibre-rich diets (10–15 per cent) may be used to help reduce obesity, and can also be used as a dietary aid in diabetic dogs, because fibre

slows the absorption of glucose, which is the end-product of carbohydrate digestion.

BONES
These contain 30 per cent calcium and 15 per cent phosphorus, magnesium and some proteins. They are deficient in fat and essential fatty acids and vitamins. Bone meal has a similar nutrient content. Be aware that too much bone in the diet will cause hard white faeces and may lead to constipation.

Never feed chicken or chop bones, as they will splinter. Fish bones can only be given to your dog if they have been pressure-cooked and are thus softened.

WATER
It is important to make sure that clean, fresh water is always available. A dog's normal daily requirement (from feeding and drinking) is about 40ml (1.4 fl oz) per kg (2.2 lb) of body weight. Water intake will obviously vary according to the temperature and the type of food you feed your dog, increasing in proportion to the amounts of dry food it consumes. Water intake also increases if a dog is suffering from ailments such as diarrhoea, diabetes or kidney disease.

▶ FEEDING YOUR DOG ◀

Select a feeding area that can be easily cleaned, and use it routinely. Use proper dog-food bowls made of stainless steel, earthenware or plastic, and wash them after each use. Serve the food at room temperature. Uneaten canned food should be disposed of immediately, but semi-moist food can be left in the bowl for several hours. Dry foods can be left out all day.

FEEDING YOUR PUPPY

A bitch's milk is rich in protein and fat, and during the first few weeks after weaning, a puppy's diet needs to reflect this. A growing puppy requires up to three times more energy intake per kg (2.2 lb) of body weight than does an adult, and because it has a limited stomach capacity it must be fed several times a day on a high-energy diet.

There are many commercial brands of specially formulated puppy foods, both grain-based and meat-based, which you should consider rather than trying to formulate your own. When a puppy is young you can also feed it milk. As a general guide, a puppy aged eight to 12 weeks should receive four meals a day of a commercial food or a home-cooked diet. You need to decide which you are going to use, and stick to it. Mixing home-cooked and commercial diets can lead to imbalances.

From three to six months, feed three meals a day. If milk appears to cause diarrhoea as your puppy gets older, it could be because of the lactose in the milk.

From six to 12 months, feed two meals a day. If you want to change the diet, introduce the new diet gradually: Day One – 25 per cent of new diet; Day Two – 50 per cent; Day Three – 75 per cent; Day Four – 100 per cent.

WARNING

Do not overfeed your puppy. If growth rate weight gain are too ra this may lead to condit such as hip dysplasia. B particularly careful if y puppy is one of the gi breeds whose growth is comparatively slow, there is evidence that heavy feeding and sup mentation may contrib to a shorter life span.

This page and opposite: *Growing, healthy puppies will enthusiastically consume their food and usually curl up and fall sleep soon afterwards.*

NUTRITION

FEEDING YOUR ADULT DOG

Most adult dogs are in the non-working, non-pregnant category, and live in temperate conditions. They can usually eat their daily ration in one meal, which satisfies their appetite better and often fits in well with a household routine. Most owners feed their dogs in the late afternoon or early evening, and after exercise. Most dogs need to urinate and defecate within an hour or two of feeding, so late-night feeding can cause problems. You can feed your dog more often to fit in with family meal times.

Large, deep-chested breeds (such as Great Danes and Irish Wolfhounds) may develop excessive gas in the stomach if fed their whole meal at once; rather divide their daily ration. If you are feeding two dogs, feed them separately and some distance apart, so a dominant dog cannot eat another's food.

HOW MUCH TO FEED

Your dog should be fed enough food to satisfy its energy needs, but no more, otherwise it will put on excess weight. The amount of energy it uses will depend not only on its activity but also on its metabolic rate. Dogs' energy needs do not increase proportionately with their body-weight: the larger the dog, the less energy per kilogram of bodyweight it needs. For example, a Chihuahua weighing 2kg/4.4 lb needs about 230 KCal (963kJ) a day, whereas a Labrador Retriever weighing 30kg/66 lb (15 times the weight) needs about 1700 KCal (7116kJ) (just over seven times the amount of energy).

If your dog is in good condition, alert and active with a healthy skin and coat, and maintaining its proper weight, it is almost certainly getting an adequate diet. If it has a scaly skin, is shedding its coat excessively, is over- or underweight, appears dull or listless, is excessively hungry or often disinterested in food, talk to your vet. You can also tell if your dog is overweight by feeling the fat layers over the ribs and spine.

Don't feed your dog household scraps between meals. Save them to become part of its normal meal, or use them as a reward. Remember that these, and treats such as chocolate drops, contain calories and it is important to make allowances for them in your dog's overall diet.

▶ NUTRITIONAL PROBLEMS ◀

These should not arise if you are feeding a properly formulated commercial diet. They may arise because a dog is:
• eating the wrong diet
• eating, but a disease is reducing its ability to absorb or use food

• not eating (anorexia) for a variety of reasons. Underfeeding results in lack of energy, weight loss and finally starvation. It could also result in a deficiency of essential nutrients. Overfeeding your dog causes obesity with its accompanying health problems.

▶ DANGER: POISON ◀

Safety around the home is just as important for pets as it is for children. Many of the plants in our gardens, as well as the substances we commonly use in the house, garden, garage or shed, can be poisonous to dogs. Puppies are particularly at risk during the stage where they chew at things, and are more likely to sample

any liquid leaking from a container. All potentially poisonous substances should be locked away, or stored safely out of a dog's reach and where a cat or other animal cannot knock them off. Substances that can give off harmful vapours should be used and stored where there is adequate ventilation.

▶ SYMPTOMS OF POISONING ◀

Consider the possibility that your dog has been poisoned if your pet is:
• crying
• panting very heavily
• drooling or foaming at the mouth
• suffering intense abdominal pain
• showing signs of shock
• collapsed or in a coma

• suddenly vomiting and/or has severe diarrhoea (more than two or three times within an hour)
• depressed
• trembling, uncoordinated, staggering or convulsing
• showing signs of an allergic reaction (swelling around the face or a red rash on the belly).

Left: *A healthy, correctly fed dog will have a shiny coat and be alert, active and energetic – quite the envy of most weary, exhausted and stressed owners.*

WHAT TO DO

- Time is critical
- Try to identify the poison
- Carry out the recommended emergency treatment described opposite
- Contact your veterinarian immediately and take your dog into the clinic
- If you have found the dog with a poisonous

or unidentified substance, take the container or packet with you. The label should contain information about the antidote and treatment for that particular type of poisoning
- If your dog has vomited, collect a specimen of the vomit in a clean container and take that with you.

▸ EMERGENCY TREATMENT ◂

If the poison is corrosive (strong acid or alkali), or if you are not sure what caused the problem:
- do not induce vomiting
- if the dog is conscious, flush the mouth and muzzle with large quantities of water, then give one tablespoon of egg white or olive oil
- take the dog to your vet immediately.

If the substance is non-corrosive, or happens to be a neurotoxin (such as snailbait):
- if the dog is conscious and has not vomited already, induce vomiting

- put the vomit material into a clean container
- take the dog and vomit material to your veterinarian immediately.

To induce vomiting, give one of the following:
- one or two large crystals of washing soda (sodium carbonate) straight down the throat
- one heaped teaspoon of table salt in warm water
- one tablespoon of mustard powder in a cup of warm water. Repeat every 10 minutes until the dog vomits.

EMERGENCY ANTIDOTES

Absorbents (absorb toxic substances): activated charcoal, up to six tablets as per package instructions, or two to three tablespoons of powder mixed in a cup of warm water.
Protectants (help to cover the stomach lining):

One tablespoon of egg white or olive oil.
Against acids: One teaspoon of bicarbonate of soda in an equal amount of water.
Against alkalis: A few teaspoons of vinegar or lemon juice in an equal amount of water.

UNDERSTANDING YOUR DOG'S BEHAVIOUR

Although dogs can live in harmony with people and have a similar social structure, their perception of their territory is very different. As a result, they interact with this territory in a very different way. If you can understand how your dog perceives its territory, you will better understand why it behaves the way it does.

▶ THE CANINE SOCIAL SYSTEM ◀

It is generally accepted that the behaviour of the domestic dog is derived from that of the wolf. Wolves live in groups, which often consist of a breeding pair and their offspring. The 'alpha' (dominant) pair asserts its dominance with dominance displays: for example, staring directly at another individual, growling or standing erect with tail up and hackles raised. The subordinate or lower-ranking wolves avoid conflict by replying with submissive behaviour, such as rolling onto the side, exposing vulnerable body parts and sometimes passing urine at the same time. Usually there is one obvious hierarchy in the females and another in the males – the alpha male always partners the alpha female.

These hierarchies are 'pyramidal' – the rank differences are most obvious between high-ranking individuals but are less distinct lower down the scale.

The alpha female is highly aggressive to other females, especially around the breeding season. The alpha male is highly aggressive towards intruders, but not so aggressive to the rest of the pack; his status is accepted and the hierarchy is maintained by deference.

A human observer may clearly distinguish the 'beta', or second in rank, male – often the most aggressive animal in the pack. Mostly, his aggression is directed towards the alpha male – when the latter animal becomes older and more vulnerable, the beta male will take over.

Wolves hunt in cooperation, but dominant animals eat before subordinates.

The cubs of the alpha pair are communally raised. The other pairs don't breed, and the entire pack will care for the offspring. This vastly increases their chances of survival.

Domestic dogs vary to differing extents from this pattern. Groups of dogs do form hierarchies,

Left: *Dogs and cats can learn to have mutual respect for each other if they are introduced to each other at a young age.*

although the visual expression of dominance is sometimes less evident. This may be because many modern breeds have facial and body characteristics that cannot change enough to communicate their attitude – think of breeds with short faces and stubby tails; it is difficult for them to posture in a typical canine fashion.

Modern dogs are more vocal than wolves, probably as a result of human selection of animals that give warning of intruders by barking, and also the selection of 'puppy type' characteristics (see p11, The development of dog types).

Top and above: *Just like wolves, dogs that are lower in the social hierarchy display submissive behaviour by tucking in their tails, rolling onto their sides or exposing vulnerable body parts.*

UNDERSTANDING YOUR DOG'S BEHAVIOUR

▶ THE DOG-HUMAN RELATIONSHIP ◀

Dogs and humans can form close associations and bonds, probably due to similarities in their social structure. Human social systems involve leaders and followers, and this order is maintained largely by deference on the part of weaker or lower-ranking individuals to those who are more powerful or skilled. The same is true of canine society.

Dogs living with humans tend to regard them as members of a pack, and soon recognize dominance and subordination in people. Consequently, it is very important to make sure that your dog is well aware of its position in your household.

Preferably, all family members should be dominant over the dog or dogs. This is usually achieved by behaving in ways that demand deference from the dog. Family members should spend time sitting on the dog's bed or in its favourite area. From puppyhood the dog should be fed at least one of its meals after the family has eaten, as this equates to the pack situation where dominant members eat first and subordinates move in later. The dog should be asked to sit and wait while people pass through doorways first. People should maintain an upright posture around the dog. If you lie on the floor and allow the dog to stand over you (as children often do in play), your dog will interpret this as subordinate behaviour – this could lead to aggression from the dog should you later try to dominate it.

Puppies that have not been given clear guidelines about their rank in the household often become aggressive at around 18 months, which is when social maturity is reached (like teenagers testing for feedback on behaviour as they mature).

Top: *When you play with your dog, maintain an upright posture as in this interaction. If you allow your dog to stand over you, it could interpret this as subordinate behaviour.*

▶ SCENT IN YOUR DOG'S WORLD ◀

The dog has the most sensitive sense of smell of all domestic animals. The nerve cells that detect scent are located in the lining of its nose, which is greatly folded and gives an area of approximately 150cm² (23 sq in) – about 30 times that of a human.

It also has a far greater concentration of scent-detecting (olfactory) cells – the number varies between breeds, reaching as high as 230 million compared to a human's five million.

As a result, some dogs can detect an odour at up to one-millionth of the concentration detectable by a human. When you walk your dog, it is moving through a world of smells, receiving messages via scent at levels as dilute as one in 10,000,000. You cannot even begin to detect them! Dogs can also detect a wider range of scents than you can. The average human can detect about 1000 types of scent, and an expert about 4000, but a dog can detect far more.

Scenting ability varies between breeds, and is best in the hounds that were developed for this purpose. The Bloodhound is one of the best: one particular animal is known to have tracked the scent trail left by a man's feet, through leather-soled boots, four and a half days after the trail had been laid.

Scent is an important means of communication for the dog. Glands that secrete odiferous substances are located around the head, neck and groin area, which is why dogs sniff at

Top: *In a dog's scent-oriented world, urine carries important messages. Dogs urinate over the spot chosen by predecessors in order to leave behind their own 'signature'.*

these areas when they meet. Two major glands (anal glands) situated on each side of the anus produce a strong-smelling secretion that coats the faeces, leaving a scent message for other dogs (which can persist for quite some time in the environment). These secretions are different in each individual. When your dog sniffs at faeces on the roadside, it is learning about the social status of whoever left the faeces and the time at which they were left.

Urine will also indicate who passed by, how long ago, and reproductive status.

THE SCENT ORGANS OF THE DOG

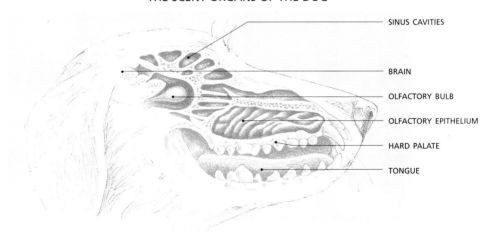

- SINUS CAVITIES
- BRAIN
- OLFACTORY BULB
- OLFACTORY EPITHELIUM
- HARD PALATE
- TONGUE

Top: *Searching for illegal drugs is only one way in which dogs serve humans with their noses. Sniffer dogs can even follow scents in search of earthquake or mountain accident victims.*

▶ SIGHT IN YOUR DOG'S WORLD ◀

A dog's vision matures at four months. Before this, many objects may appear blurred, which could explain the apparently unprovoked fearful behaviour seen in some puppies.

In most breeds, the eyes are set to the side of the head, so their binocular vision is over a narrower field than ours (about 20° less). The degree of binocular vision varies between breeds because of variations in the positions of the eyes. Although dogs' binocular vision is not as good as ours, they have much wider peripheral vision (about 70° more), which gives them a greater awareness of movement. They can detect movements so subtle that they would have to be magnified 10 times before a human could see them. Visual signals are important in canine communication. Posture, ear position, tail position, and movement and hair pattern communicate mood and intention.

A dog will react to subtle changes in body language that you don't even notice. This may explain why your dog growls at an approaching stranger. Their body language may appear normal to you, but threatening to the dog.

Dogs have rudimentary colour vision that allows them to pick out objects based on colour – shades of colour, however, are not well discriminated.

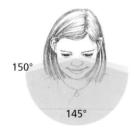

150°

145°

A HUMAN SEES FROM SIDE-TO-SIDE – A TOTAL OF 150°– OF WHICH 145° IS BINOCULAR OVERLAP.

275°

130°

A CAT SEES FROM SIDE-TO-SIDE – A TOTAL OF 275°– OF WHICH 130° IS BINOCULAR OVERLAP.

250–290°

80–110°

A DOG HAS A TOTAL VISION OF 250–290°, OF WHICH 80–110° IS OVERLAP – MUCH LESS THAN HUMANS.

Top: *There's no need to pick a particularly bright frisbee for your dog: shades of brightness are not readily discerned, but the movement is easily followed.*

Communication using sound is important for dogs, especially in situations where vision is impaired, such as in thick undergrowth. Dogs make a number of different noises, such as whining, barking, growling, howling and grunting, which are used in different contexts.

Compared to humans, dogs have far better hearing. Sound travels in waves, where frequency is measured in units called Hertz (Hz). The higher the frequency, the higher the pitch of the sound.

The average human has a hearing range of 20–20,000Hz. Dogs, on the other hand, have a range of about 20–65,000Hz. They are most sensitive in the range 500–16,000Hz. One reason why some dogs (and cats) dislike the sound of vacuum cleaners or certain two-stroke engines could be that the machines emit disturbing high-pitched sounds that we as humans cannot hear.

The magnitude (loudness) of sounds is measured in decibels (dB) – zero decibels start at the threshold of human hearing. Very loud noise can 'hurt' your ears, and the pain threshold for humans is 120dB.

Because a dog's hearing is more acute, they can hear much fainter sounds than humans can. For example, a sound just audible to a human standing 6m (20ft) away from its source can be heard by most dogs at a distance of 25m (80ft). Dogs pick up the sound of an approaching thunderstorm 10km (6 miles) away much sooner than we can.

The dog's acute hearing adds to its value as a guard dog and enables it to obey commands over long distances. It may also explain why a dog may appear restless and bark for no apparent reason.

Dogs are very sensitive to voice tone, and respond best to a quiet, 'happy' voice. Use a light, soft voice for praise and a gruff or loud tone for commands or correction. Words used for praise or commands should be short, simple and clear (see pp72–85, Training your dog).

A sound stimulus is reduced in effect if accompanied by touching a dog's body, as the physical stimulus overrides the auditory command, so don't pat or touch your dog while you are giving it a command.

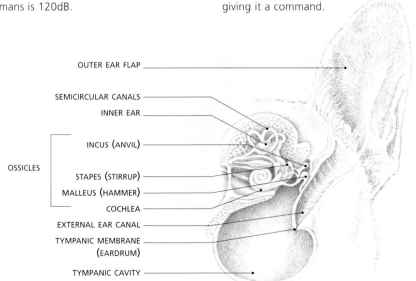

OUTER EAR FLAP

SEMICIRCULAR CANALS

INNER EAR

INCUS (ANVIL)

OSSICLES

STAPES (STIRRUP)

MALLEUS (HAMMER)

COCHLEA

EXTERNAL EAR CANAL

TYMPANIC MEMBRANE
(EARDRUM)

TYMPANIC CAVITY

Above: *Most dogs, such as this German Shepherd, have such a keen sense of hearing that they can detect faint sounds 25m (27yd) away.*

UNDERSTANDING YOUR DOG'S BEHAVIOUR

A dog's brain is the control centre for its body and, as such, is responsible for monitoring its behaviour. The main part of the brain influencing behaviour is the limbic system which features the brain stem and the prefrontal cortex. More specifically, the limbic system is the entire circuitry that controls your dog's emotional behaviour and motivational drive. The parts controlling your dog's behaviour are the:

- Amygdala: Control of aggression, fear and tameness. It enables social cues to be picked up and is a key factor in memory and food intake. This part of the brain is the emotional control centre.
- Cingulate gyrus: Coordinates smell and sight. It is the interceptor of pain and aggression, and regulates tameness and motivation.
- Hippocampus: Long-term memory, spatial awareness and three-dimensional mapping.
- Hypothalamus: Important in fight/flight response, sexual behaviour, appetite, thirst, pleasure and rage.

- Locus coereleus: This is the control of anxiety-based responses and arousal.
- Neocortex: Important in memory.
- Olfactory bulb: Sensory processing (scent is known to trigger memories).
- Raphe nuclei: A combination of nuclei which house most of the serotonin-containing neurons. This controls mood and emotion, and coordinates sleep/wake cycles with the locus coereleus.
- Thalamus: A relay centre; important in sexual orientation, and emotional and physical safety.

Neurotransmitters are chemical messengers, and various brain regions contain their receptors. Neurotransmitters important in behaviour include serotonin, GABA (calming), adrenalin, acetylcholine and dopamine (excitatory). These act to excite or calm the brain and thus influence behaviour. Some animals, for example, have insufficient calming neurotransmitters and exhibit anxiety-based behavioural abnormalities that require medication to rectify.

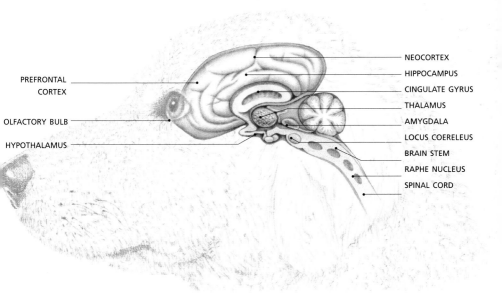

TRAINING YOUR DOG

Most aspiring dog owners dream of the perfect canine companion: obedient, quiet and well behaved in public. Unfortunately for some, the dream is soon shattered. Their beloved pet takes them for a walk, covers their good clothes with muddy paw prints, chases cats, bowls over elderly pedestrians and cannot be left alone in the car in case it demolishes the upholstery.

How can you avoid finding yourself in this situation? The answer is to start training your puppy as soon as it becomes part of the household.

Remember, though, that dog training must be a partnership. It is not just the dog that needs training, but you and your family as well. It is no good if one member of your family is able to handle a dog properly while none of the others can. All members of your family must be dominant over the dog, although it may single out one individual as its pack leader.

▶ PUPPY PRESCHOOL ◀

These preschools are usually held in selected areas of veterinary clinics that are free from any possible contamination. They are designed to allow young puppies to socialize in a safe, disease-free environment and to help owners begin training as soon as they bring the puppy home, usually at the age of seven or eight weeks. There is strong evidence to show that puppies that have attended preschool are far more obedient and easier to handle than those that have not.

If possible, join a puppy preschool as soon as you get the puppy and spend at least 10 minutes twice a day reinforcing and practising what you learn each week.

Once you have completed puppy preschool, keep at your daily practice sessions. By this time your puppy will have had all its vaccinations and you will be taking it out and about. Practise all your training at regular intervals during walks, too.

If you want to complete further training, locate a reputable dog training centre (see p82, Advanced training).

Inset: *A soft harness and leash for puppies and small dogs.*
Left: *Constantly reinforcing your basic training commands makes for an obedient dog that is a pleasure to walk and exercise in a public area.*

Puppy preschool will offer basic training, but you may wish to start training your dog at home while you are waiting for the preschool term to begin. Puppies learn very quickly from eight weeks of age. Most puppies can master the five easiest commands – 'sit', 'stay', 'come', 'down' and 'heel' – by the time they are three months old.

Most puppies will work for food treats. Dried liver is popular and is produced commercially in wafer-thin strips. Puppies that don't like liver may work for cheese or biscuits.

It is best to use treats all the time in the early stages of training. Gradually, you can use them intermittently and eventually phase them out, rewarding with praise only.

THE BASIC COMMANDS

Teach the commands in the order in which they are listed below, as 'sit' is usually the most easily learned command, and 'come' is the most difficult. It is best to train a puppy on a lead.

SIT
Stand in front of the puppy, hold a treat above its head, just about at ear level. Ask it to sit. To get the treat the puppy needs to put its head up and back, and in doing this it will naturally place its bottom on the ground. As soon as this happens, give it the treat and praise it.

Some puppies will walk backwards instead of sitting. If you have this problem, stand the puppy in a corner before asking it to sit. Most learn very quickly and can sit well after only one week of training.

DOWN
Ask the puppy to sit and reward it when it does so. Hold another reward in your hand and move it between the puppy's front legs and under its chest, giving the command 'down'. In following the treat with its nose the puppy will move into a lying position. When it has done this, release the treat and praise the puppy.

Some puppies only get half way to the ground at first. If this happens, use your free hand to gently push the puppy on the shoulder until it lies down.

STAY
Ask the puppy to sit or lie down. Then stand beside it and place one hand flat in front of its face. Give the command 'stay', take one step forward, stop, then step back again and praise the puppy.

Very gradually increase the number of steps you take away from the puppy. If the puppy moves, say 'no', place it straight back in position and ask it to stay again. In two to three weeks, practising daily, the puppy should stay happily while you walk to the opposite end of the room and return to it.

HEEL
From its sitting position, encourage the puppy to look up at you by holding a treat in your clenched hand and talking in an 'interesting' voice (varying the tone and pitch and saying things that will make you feel very silly!). Walk forward, give the command 'heel', and encour-

Inset: *A harness for a medium-sized dog.*

age the puppy to follow while still looking up at you. Always keep the lead loose. Keep repeating 'heel, good dog, look'. When the puppy is walking freely looking up, give it a reward but keep walking while you do so. This reinforces that the reward is for walking well. If you stop to give the reward, the puppy will associate stopping with a treat and will soon refuse to move!

COME

Practise this frequently throughout the day in various situations. Always carry treats. Call the puppy by name, followed by the command 'come', and reward it with a treat when it comes to you. When you call, you need to sound interesting enough to override the rest of the environment.

SIT: TELL YOUR PUPPY TO 'SIT', MOTIONING IT DOWNWARDS WITH A TREAT JUST ABOVE EAR LEVEL. THEN REWARD IT WITH THE TREAT AND PRAISE.

DOWN: TELL YOUR PUPPY TO 'SIT', THEN REWARD IT. NEXT, MOVE A TREAT BETWEEN THE PUPPY'S FRONT LEGS AND UNDER ITS CHEST, GIVING THE COMMAND 'DOWN'. GIVE THE PUPPY THE TREAT AND PRAISE IT.

STAY: TELL YOUR PUPPY TO 'SIT' AND THEN 'STAY', USING A TREAT AND PRAISE. REPEAT THE 'STAY' COMMAND AND STEP AWAY. REPEAT THE PROCESS ONCE MORE.

HEEL: ENCOURAGE THE SITTING PUPPY TO LOOK AT YOU BY HOLDING A TREAT. THEN WALK AND ENCOURAGE IT TO FOLLOW, REPEATING THE COMMAND 'HEEL'. GIVE IT A TREAT WHILE IT IS WALKING FREELY, LOOKING UP.

When the puppy comes to you, treat it as the most wonderful event of the day. You have to make it worth the puppy's while to return to you when there are so many other interesting things in the surroundings to investigate.

Always take young puppies and dogs out on an extending lead and do not let them run totally free in public areas until you know they will return. This can take up to a year of training. It is one of the most difficult lessons for the puppy.

It is essential that you never, ever punish the puppy for not returning. If it ignores you, quietly go and get it (if you are working free at home in an enclosed space) or reel in the extending lead. Ask the puppy to sit, then reward and praise it for that. Have a game, and make following you fun. Keep trying and eventually your perseverance will be rewarded.

QUIET

Some dogs have a tendency to bark at the slightest provocation. It is useful to teach these dogs a 'quiet' command.

Start this training when the dog is sitting or lying quietly. Praise it and say 'quiet'. Do this frequently through the day. When the dog barks at something, call it to you, ask it to sit, then tell it to be quiet. Praise and reward it for being quiet.

Dogs naturally bark at unfamiliar sounds or intruders, and this command will control barking, but not extinguish their desire to bark.

FETCH

Some dog breeds are natural retrievers, while others just do not see the point. This should be evident from about 12 weeks old if your puppy is going to enjoy retrieving – it will naturally pick up objects and invite you to chase it while holding something in its mouth. If you throw something such as a ball, your puppy will chase it and try to pick it up.

You need to work with this natural retrieve drive to teach the dog to fetch an object on command and to relinquish it to you. Begin by encouraging the puppy to chase a toy that is hand held, then thrown a short distance. Go with the puppy, pick up the toy, give it to the puppy and take the puppy back to the starting point. Give the command 'fetch'. Initially, work with the puppy on an extending lead so that you have control over its movements.

Some puppies retrieve the object but then refuse to give it up afterwards. You can overcome this by swapping the retrieved object for a treat or a brief play with a favourite toy. Eventually, the fun of having an object thrown for chasing is enough reward to encourage puppy to give up the object.

Breeds that are natural retrievers include the 'bird' dogs such as Labradors, Pointers, Setters and Poodles. Other breeds that like to retrieve include German Shepherd Dogs, Dalmatians, most Terriers and many cross-breeds.

Top: *The 'sit' command is easiest to learn and, therefore, usually the first one taught. A puppy will respond enthusiastically to postive learning experiences and, by the age of three months, should obey 'stay' as well.*

Puppies often bite in play with people, just as they do with other puppies. This play-biting can become quite difficult to cope with, especially in puppies that do not attend a puppy preschool.

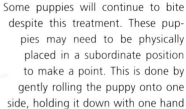

During puppy play, if one puppy bites another too hard, the bitten puppy will cry out sharply and will immediately turn its back on the biter and refuse to interact further. If pushed, it may growl or snap at the biter, but this is not usually necessary. Usually the biter will appear shocked by the other puppy's reaction and will back off. Further approaches will be gentler. If your puppy bites you, say 'ouch!' loudly and walk away. Ignore the biting puppy or, if possible, leave the room for five minutes. Return, call the puppy, and ask it to sit and then pat it. If it bites again, repeat the process. Your puppy will soon discover that biting causes it to be left alone and ignored.

Some puppies will continue to bite despite this treatment. These puppies may need to be physically placed in a subordinate position to make a point. This is done by gently rolling the puppy onto one side, holding it down with one hand and holding its mouth closed with the other, while looking directly into its eyes. When the puppy stops struggling, release it and stroke it gently. Repeat this procedure whenever the puppy bites hard and refuses to stop. It is probably a good idea to ask your veterinarian or behaviourist to demonstrate this before you attempt it yourself.

Avoid 'roughing up the puppy' as an attempt to play. This will only encourage the puppy to bite and play roughly. If you must indulge in tugging and growling games, use a tug toy and do not allow the puppy to latch onto your sleeves, trousers or any of your clothing.

Inset: *A soft muzzle can be used on walks and during training sessions to prevent your dog from biting others.*
Above: *It is perfectly natural for your dogs to indulge in tugging and growling games.*

▶ JUMPING UP ◀

Some dogs become very excited when visitors arrive or when owners return home, and express this by jumping up at the person or people present. This can be irritating and may result in clothing being torn or damaged – and, of course, it may result in young children or frail older people being knocked over.

If your dog jumps up, turn right away and walk in the opposite direction. Do not speak to the dog and, if possible, leave the room and shut in the dog. Return to the dog and immediately ask it to sit. Reward the sit with a treat. If it jumps up again, say 'no'. Ask it to sit and again reward the sit. If the dog jumps and manages to get its paws onto you, turn away again without touching the dog, so that it falls to the ground. Request it to sit again and reward the dog.

If the dog insists on jumping despite this protocol, enlist help. Arrange for someone to visit at a prearranged time. Have the dog on a head halter and lead, and prevent the dog from jumping at the visitor. Command the dog to sit calmly while the visitor enters the house and greets you. The visitor should ignore the dog at first. Reward the dog for quiet behaviour, then allow the visitor to greet the dog while it is sitting calmly. If it makes any attempt to jump, the visitor should stop petting it and walk away. Once the dog is sitting quietly, the visitor may return and pet the dog.

Family members can help each other in a similar way if the dog is a problem every time someone returns home. Dogs soon learn that they will be ignored or shut away if they jump, and will usually change their behaviour to running up and sitting in front of a visitor or their returning owner.

Preventing jumping up:
- do not encourage puppies to stand up on you or jump up at you for attention
- don't be overexuberant in greeting your dog or puppy
- command the dog to sit or lie down before you give it attention.

Top: *Your dog's training should always be based on reward and positive reinforcement.*

▶ REPRIMAND AND CORRECTION ◀

Modern training techniques rarely involve physical correction: their emphasis is on redirecting unacceptable behaviour and rewarding correct behaviour. This is known as positive reinforcement.

'Traditional' methods of hitting dogs with rolled up newspapers or slapping them may result in hand-shy, confused dogs. In most cases the dog is not deliberately behaving badly. Your dog cannot easily tell the difference between the old sneaker that it is allowed to play with and your expensive shoes. Patient redirection to its own toys will be more successful than shouting and hitting the dog.

If you really feel physical correction is indicated and redirection has not worked – for example, if the dog insists on cornering the cat or tearing up the cushions – then the following 'correction procedure' is far better than striking the animal:

• take hold of it firmly by the collar
• look directly into its eyes
• say 'no' firmly
• banish it to another room
• return to the dog in two minutes, request a 'sit' or 'down', and reward it.

A water pistol may also be used to correct this sort of behaviour. Squirt the dog full in the face while it is performing the behaviour. When it jumps back in surprise, call it to you, request a sit and reward it.

In most cases, if the dog has been properly trained as a puppy using redirection and reward, physical correction should not be required.

Remember that there are veterinarians and behaviourists that specialize in behaviour problems. If you are having difficulty with training your dog, or if it is aggressive, pushy, noisy, excessively fearful or anxious, help is available.

▶ TRAINING AIDS ◀

Your puppy should be fitted a soft puppy collar as soon as it has settled into your home. Start by putting the collar on for short periods at a time when your puppy is playing or eating, then gradually extend its use until it is being worn all the time.

Once the puppy is used to the collar, clip on a lightweight, 120cm (47in) leash. Practise walking the puppy around for a short period, when necessary using a gentle pull to steer it in the right direction. Try to keep your puppy on your left side, holding the handle of the leash in your right hand. Be patient while the puppy gets used to this, and use lots of praise and rewards when it does things right. If the puppy resents the leash, try leaving it clipped to its collar, trailing behind the puppy for short periods – just remember to follow the puppy to make sure the lead doesn't catch on anything or end up being chewed.

Once your puppy is used to walking with you around the garden on a collar and lead, try a trip around the neighbourhood. Forget about making the puppy walk on your left side, as it is now being exposed to new experiences and

Inset: *A soft nylon, quick-release collar and lead for a medium-sized dog.*

should be allowed some freedom to investigate.

A long leash (lead) is important, because the dog can investigate the environment while safely under your control. Keeping it on a tight leash may cause it to back away rather than follow you willingly.

STANDARD LEADS AND COLLARS

From six months onwards, adolescent and adult dogs may wear broad nylon or leather collars. It is wise to attach an identity disc to these.

Choose a lead that is suitable for the size and strength of your dog. For a large breed it is better to have a fairly short, strong lead, with the handle made of leather plus a chain attachment to the collar, or a short rolled-leather lead. For a small breed you can use a thinner, longer lead made of leather or nylon.

EXPANDING LEADS

These come in a range of sizes correlated to the weight of the dog. They provide a lead length of 3–5m (10–15ft) and are ideal for training young dogs to return when called, as they allow controlled freedom.

Important: It is best not to use any of the following aids, such as head halters, harnesses and chokers, without expert advice. Check

Top: *Once your dog can walk sensibly alongside you, you may wish to consider a more advanced training programme for it.*

with your veterinarian as to which, if any, is appropriate for your dog. Make sure that you take the dog in for a proper fitting and to get instructions on how to use it.

HEAD HALTERS

Some dogs insist on pulling when on a leash, which makes walking them unpleasant. Head halters are designed to allow you to control the dog's head, and therefore its speed and direction.

Head halters are also useful in helping you to avoid aggressive encounters between dogs. With a halter you can turn your dog's head away from an approaching dog. This should stop any aggression because you are placing your dog into a submissive posture.

Warning: If you wish to control your dog with a head halter you must learn to use it properly. Tugging too hard could cause damage to your dog's neck.

CHECK, CHOKER OR SLIP-CHAINS

These are chains that are looped to form a slip-noose effect. The idea is to tighten the chain with a short, sharp jerk and immediately release it. The dog learns to associate the noise of the chain with discomfort if it pulls, so it walks without pulling. Chains with large links are preferable to those with small links.

The trouble is that many people link the choker incorrectly. Have your veterinarian show you the right way. Another problem is that dogs ignore the sound and pull hard on the chain. When they do this, the chain tightens and they literally choke themselves. Double-action slip-chains are also available, which tighten only a little and do not choke the dog. Or you can use a slip-collar made of leather, cord or a broad strip of nylon.

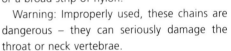

Warning: Improperly used, these chains are dangerous – they can seriously damage the throat or neck vertebrae.

HARNESSES

These are designed to fit around the dog's chest and behind its front legs. They can be very useful for small dogs, especially those with short faces, or for dogs that have had neck injuries. A standard harness is useless on a large dog with a tendency to pull; rather choose a 'no-pull' harness, designed to put pressure on the dog's chest and to pull its front leg back when it pulls. It is usually quite effective, although it can cause chafing.

CITRONELLA COLLARS

These collars are fitted with a device that sprays citronella into the dog's face each time it barks. Such a collar can be useful in cases where you are experiencing nuisance barking in your pet. It is important, though, that the dog be assessed by a behaviourist before one is used, and then the collar should at first be used only under supervision. If the barking is anxiety-related, using a citronella collar will make the dog much worse.

Inset top: *A choker, also known as a check or slip-chain, for a medium-sized dog.*
Inset left: *A soft clip-on collar and lead for a small to medium-sized dog.*

▶ ADVANCED TRAINING ◀

Once it has mastered the basic commands, you will have a dog that is manageable and fun to be with. You can then build on these and teach distance commands, such as asking the dog to obey 'down' from a distance. Dog training clubs can help you with advanced training, and your veterinary clinic should be able to provide good recommendations.

SOME BREEDS IDEAL FOR WORKING, OBEDIENCE OR AGILITY TRIALS

- Bearded Collie
- Belgian Shepherd
- Border Collie
- Boxer
- Dalmatian
- Doberman
- German Shepherd Dog (Alsatian)
- Golden Retriever
- Great Dane
- Irish Setter
- Labrador Retriever
- Old English Sheepdog
- Pointer
- Poodle
- Rottweiler
- Schnauzer
- Weimaraner
- Welsh Corgi

▶ TRAINING THE ADULT DOG ◀

If you adopt a dog from a rescue centre or from a breeding kennel, you will be faced with training an adult animal. It may have bad habits that have been established over months or years. Time, effort and patience will be required to retrain it to behave in a way that is acceptable to you, but it can be done. For example, police dogs often do not begin training until they are 20 months of age.

In general, the training will be little different from that used with puppies, although you should follow the same protocols for the various commands as described for puppy training.

Be aware, though, that the dog may have had some prior training and may respond to different commands, so play with words for a while and evaluate the response. For example, some dogs lie down to a 'drop' command, while others respond to 'down' or 'lie down'.

Difficulties may arise if a command has become obsolete. This happens where people use a command but do not ensure that a suitable response occurs. The dog then learns to ignore the command. This commonly occurs with 'no' and 'come'. In such cases it is often better to use alternative words to train the dog to respond; you might decide to use 'stop' and 'here' instead.

Inset: *A leather collar, a strong yet soft cloth leash and a choker chain for a large dog.*

Once you have decided on a particular command, ensure that a response always occurs. Keep your new dog on a retractable lead until you are confident that it responds well to your chosen commands.

House training can be a major problem with some adult dogs. Those that have been in breeding kennels for long periods may have become used to defecating on concrete (they have developed a 'substrate preference') and as a result will soil footpaths, driveways and doorsteps, to your and the neighbours' annoyance. If there is a solid surface indoors these dogs may be stimulated to defecate on it, too.

You need to change their substrate preference. The only way to do this is to keep a strict eye on such a dog, take it outside on a lead whenever it is likely to need to relieve itself, stay with it, and praise it when it has obliged in a suitable area.

Do not expect your dog to know what is expected of it automatically. Just because it is an adult doesn't mean it comes ready-programmed to suit your requirements! Don't demand too much too soon and be understanding if it makes mistakes.

Top: *Large dogs require more space, time and patience when being trained and exercised.*

Most dogs of either sex have some tendency to guard their home territory. Motivation to guard varies between breeds. Rottweilers, German Shepherd Dogs, Dobermans and Rhodesian Ridgebacks are among those most likely to guard. Males tend to guard at a higher intensity than females.

Most people feel secure with a dog that will warn them of the presence of an intruder by barking. A dog may be encouraged to do this by the owner reacting to noises outside the house. If the owner jumps up, goes to the door and says to the dog 'What's that, what's that?' or makes a hissing noise, the dog will be encouraged to bark whenever it hears a strange noise. Dogs that have been trained to obey voice commands should stop reacting to an intruder when reassured or given the commands 'sit' or 'quiet' by their owner.

Dogs may be trained to attack on command, but this is not something the general public should need or wish to do. Training dogs in this

Top left: *Police dogs receive specialized training and need to be courageous and intelligent.*
Top right: *If you want your dog to be trained to attack on command, and are prepared to risk legal action, you will need to find a professional trainer.*

area is a specialized, professional job. There are some people who want to have dogs that attack intruders on sight. In most cases these dogs are kept in outdoor compounds and are encouraged to react without any control at the first sign of intrusion. These dogs are allowed to bite anyone entering the area. They are potentially dangerous and owners risk legal action if a person is injured. These dogs cannot tell the difference between someone calling at the property for legitimate reasons and someone with evil intent. All intruders will be bitten.

▶ THE ARRIVAL OF A NEW BABY ◀

About two months prior to the baby's arrival, or as soon as you have set up the nursery, introduce your dog to the equipment and toys that will be part of the nursery scene. Allow it to become familiar with the scent of the talcs and lotions you will be using on your newborn, and to the sounds of squeaky toys and musical night-lights.

While you are away in hospital after the birth, send used baby clothes home with your partner and let the dog sniff at these to become familiar with their scent. When you bring the infant home, leave it in the car while you greet your dog alone. Leash the dog, ask your partner to hold it and bring in the infant. Allow the dog to sniff the infant and to accompany you into the nursery while you settle your new child into its crib.

In the days that follow, allow the dog to be involved with all the baby care. It is best to have it tied up close by in the room while you are busy changing or feeding. Never leave the dog and infant together unsupervised. Infants move and sound like prey and can evoke predatory aggression in some dogs (see p92, Predatory aggression).

Above: *While toddlers and dogs can become the best of friends, it is essential that you never leave an infant and a dog alone together.*

COMMON BEHAVIOURAL PROBLEMS

▶ AGGRESSION ◀

In the canine world, aggression is part of normal behaviour. Dogs display aggression when threatened by another animal, during hunting, when protecting their young and when establishing a social order, and show it by adopting various postures accompanied by vocalizations such as growling, snarling and barking. Aggression between dogs may be counteracted by submissive behaviour by the weaker or lower ranking animal. This helps to avoid serious fights.

Aggression can become a problem when it is excessive, or directed towards people. In fact, it is one of the most common behavioural problems seen in dogs.

DOMINANCE AGGRESSION

This is the most common type of aggression problem and occurs when a dog tries to enforce its will on its owners, challenging them for control. The dog may already feel that it is in control, or it may be testing its owner to get some feedback on its standing in the household.

Dominantly aggressive dogs commonly growl or snap at their owners if they are disturbed while sleeping, or asked to move from a specific spot or to obey a command that does not appeal to them. This form of aggression is usually first seen when the dog reaches social maturity, at the age of 18 months to two years. At this age the animal needs to know where it stands in the hierarchy of the household and will attempt to establish a 'rank'. As a result, it may growl at some members of a family but not others. Children are usually the first to be challenged, probably because they are small and less assertive in manner than adults.

Dogs with dominance aggression may also show possessive aggression and/or food aggression (see p90).

If your dog is behaving in an aggressive manner towards you or members of your family, you should seek the help of your veterinarian. He or she may then refer you to an animal behaviour specialist.

The dog must have a preliminary health check to make sure that there is no underlying health

Left: *Locked in; some dogs do not cope well being separated from their owners.*

problem causing the change in behaviour. If the dog is diagnosed with dominance aggression, there are special behaviour modification programmes that need to be followed. These are usually highly successful, but require time, effort and motivation on the owner's part.

PREVENTING DOMINANCE AGGRESSION

You can reduce the risk of your dog developing dominance aggression by providing it with clear guidelines for acceptable behaviour from puppyhood. Here are some helpful guidelines:

- Feed your puppy its evening meal after the family has eaten. This reinforces the family's dominance over the puppy. In a pack situation, dominant animals eat first.

- Make sure that you sit on your puppy's bed for a short while every day, to assert your dominance over it.

- Begin training as soon as you get the puppy, by attending puppy preschool.

- If the puppy shows signs of aggression, give it timeout for five or 10 minutes in a separate room. Play with it only when it is behaving non-aggressively.

- Require that the puppy allow family members to walk through doorways ahead of it.

- Spend five or 10 minute daily on training.

- Insist on 'sit' and 'down' at least twice daily once the puppy has mastered these commands.

- Do not give in to pawing for attention. Ignore it and provide attention only when the puppy is quiet or has earned attention by sitting when asked.

Above: *Play fights are a method of establishing which dog is the dominant one, without causing serious injury.*

COMMON BEHAVIOUR PROBLEMS

STATES OF AGGRESSION RESPONSE

NORMAL DOCILE SATE

BEGINNINGS OF AGGRESSION

INCREASED AGGRESSION

FIERCE AGGRESSION

STATES OF AGGRESSION AND FEAR RESPONSE

BEGINNINGS OF FEAR

INCREASED FEARFUL RESPONSE

AGGRESSION AND FEAR

FEAR AND EXTREME AGGRESSION

FEAR AGGRESSION

This is the second-most common type of aggression, and in some cases it is inherited. Fear aggression is most common in dogs adopted from animal shelters and often stems from past abuses. These animals require rehabilitation.

Dogs with fear aggression may start to show typical behaviour patterns from three months. They appear scared even when there is nothing to trigger the fear. When out walking they may appear terrified of an approaching pedestrian, or of an object on the roadside. They respond by growling, shaking, tucking their tails between their legs, backing away from the object or person, and possibly urinating or defecating. The hair on their neck and rump will usually be erect. With these animals it is important to seek help from an animal behaviour specialist. They often require medication and a programme of desensitization, which may involve gradual exposure to the triggering stimuli, in conjunction with relaxation therapy. In the meanwhile, you could try these temporary measures:

- avoid contact with stimuli that trigger a fear response until help can be found
- don't reward the fearful behaviour by patting and reassuring the dog. If it starts to behave fearfully, ignore it
- when the dog starts to relax, reward the relaxed behaviour.

PREVENTING FEAR AGGRESSION

It is probably impossible to prevent fear aggression completely when dealing with genetically predisposed animals. Early exposure to different environments and people – and positive experiences associated with these – may help.

POSSESSIVE AGGRESSION

A typical example is a dog that refuses to relinquish toys or objects stolen from its owners. When pressed to return these items, it may growl, snarl and even bite. Dogs showing possessive aggression often also show dominance aggression. The possessive aggression is considered to be part of a 'control complex' in these animals.

Possessive aggression is potentially dangerous, especially where young children are associating with the animal. Your behaviourist can recommend a programme for treatment, and until you have completed that programme it is safer not to meet the dog's challenge.

PREVENTING POSSESSIVE AGGRESSION

These tactics are sure to help:
- ensure that puppies are given a clear understanding of their subordinate position in the household (see p87, Dominance aggression)
- avoid playing fighting games over toys with young puppies or older dogs
- teach puppies to relinquish balls or toys in exchange for rewards.

FOOD AGGRESSION

Dogs showing food aggression may be very dangerous, especially for young children. These dogs savagely defend their food and growl constantly while eating. If they have a bone or a biscuit, they will sometimes even lunge at and bite anyone who passes close to them. Food aggression may occur in conjunction with dominance aggression. It is probably easiest and safest to feed these dogs in a separate and enclosed room. Avoid giving them bones as these are usually very actively defended. It is possible, but often difficult, to train animals with this tendency out of their behaviour, so seek the help of an expert.

Above: *It is natural for dogs to jealously guard their food or bones and fight for larger portions.*

Start by asking the dog to sit at a distance from its empty food bowl. Pick up the empty bowl, place a little food in it, place it on the ground and allow the dog to eat. When the dog has finished, repeat the process. Eventually you should be able to hold the bowl while the dog eats from it. If the dog growls during any part of the procedure, stop the feeding.

PREVENTING FOOD AGGRESSION

It is normal behaviour for dogs to want to protect their food. Puppies in large litters may rapidly learn to fight for a larger portion, and to guard whatever they have. It may be helpful to hand feed your new puppy frequently from its own bowl and to sit nearby while it eats. Ensure that your dog knows that you are dominant.

MATERNAL AGGRESSION

This may occur close to, or immediately after whelping. Bitches will savagely defend their puppies in response to any intrusion, and on occasion have even killed their puppies. Maternal aggression may also occur during false pregnancy when toys will be fiercely protected

instead. Try these tactics to deal with a bitch showing signs of maternal aggression:
- try to avoid disturbing the bitch during the first week of motherhood
- from then on, call the bitch out of the room, attach a lead and take her out to walk while

Top: *Maternal aggression decreases in intensity as the puppies get older.*

someone else changes the bedding
- feed her on return and leave her alone
- in cases of false pregnancy, remove the nest and toys while the bitch is out walking. Alter her daily routine and provide new interests. Some bitches may need to be taken to the vet for hormone treatment.

PREVENTING MATERNAL AGGRESSION
Bitches showing signs of maternal aggression should be spayed. They are likely to behave this way with future litters, and having them spayed is the only solution to preventing this problem, as there appears to be an inherited tendency for such behaviour.

PREDATORY AGGRESSION

Dogs prone to predatory aggression will develop a habit of stalking and killing other animals, such as cats, squirrels and even chickens, sheep and goats. In most cases this is done silently and swiftly. Not only is this highly undesirable behaviour, as these dogs will kill neighbours' pets as well as wildlife, it is also a potential threat for humans.

The worst possible situation is when such a dog begins to focus its attention on young children and babies in the household. To the dog, newborn and young babies appear to be behaving like wounded prey: they are uncoordinated and prone to sudden high-pitched screaming. Such actions may trigger a dog's predatory behaviour.

PREVENTING PREDATORY AGGRESSION
A dog showing this behaviour cannot be trained out of it, and must be under control at all times. Good obedience training will help to control these animals, but they can't be trusted to be alone with possible victims, and should never be left unsupervised around children.

Below: *Highly dangerous predatory aggression can be controlled with obedience training.*

REDIRECTED AGGRESSION

This behaviour is seen when a dog is prevented from doing something aggressive that its owners consider inappropriate: for example, growling at a visitor or terrorizing the postman. Immediately after it has been reprimanded the dog chases the cat or threatens a family member.

The most important thing with this type of aggression is to identify what triggers the behaviour and deal with that. If the dog bites the cat every time it is told off for chasing the postman, then it is best for everyone if the dog learns not to chase the person who delivers the post. This involves a process of desensitization to his or her arrival. In order to achieve this, the dog is taught to associate the postal deliverer with another behaviour, such as 'sit and concentrate on the owner', in return for a food reward. A behaviourist will help you with a protocol designed for your dog.

PREVENTING REDIRECTED AGGRESSION

It is probably impossible to predict if an animal will show redirected aggression. Thorough obedience training should help to decrease the likelihood of this behaviour occurring.

If a dog shows signs of inappropriate aggression towards any other animal or person, squirting it with a water pistol may help diffuse the situation until a behaviour modification programme can be started.

IDIOPATHIC AGGRESSION

'Idiopathic' means of unknown cause. Some dogs may suddenly, and for no obvious reason, have violent aggressive outbursts. Such dogs may foam at the mouth during these outbursts and cannot be distracted or safely approached.

It is likely there is some underlying mental defect, and this is a difficult condition to deal with. These dogs are best shut away during such outbursts, and may require sedation. In some instances, your vet may suggest euthanasia.

Top: *Inter-dog aggression is a common problem on walks – it may be due to underlying anxiety in one or other of the dogs.*

PREVENTING IDIOPATHIC AGGRESSION

This type of behaviour cannot be predicted, as there are usually no obvious triggers, so it is impossible to prevent, unfortunately. The condition is relatively rare, however.

AGGRESSION TOWARDS STRANGE DOGS

This commonly causes problems on walks. Two dogs, on or off leashes, meet and begin to fight. An aggressive dog will challenge any dog that crosses its path, regardless of the age, sex or size of the perceived opponent.

If the other dog is extremely submissive, the situation may be diffused. If not, despite a submissive display by the other dog, there may be a seriously aggressive encounter.

This is frightening for the owners of both dogs, and often physically damaging to the dogs involved. Dogs that are overtly aggressive are behaving abnormally, and this may be due to an underlying anxiety, and a lack of certain chemicals in the brain.

Where this behaviour occurs in male dogs, castration may be helpful. It will not solve the problem, but will help decrease the dog's reactivity.

It is helpful to walk an aggressive dog in a head halter (see p81). This ensures that you have control of the dog's head. When another dog approaches, turn your dog's head to the side. This puts it in a submissive posture with the neck exposed and prevents aggressive signalling.

There are desensitization programmes which may be used to modify this behaviour. Aggressive dogs are taught to relax and concentrate on their owners in the presence of other dogs. Your behaviourist will be able to help you with this.

PREVENTING AGGRESSION TOWARDS STRANGE DOGS

- Castration: this decreases the level of aggression in males.
- Adequate socialization of dogs from puppyhood: dogs that have socialized regularly and positively with other dogs from puppyhood, and continue to do so through adulthood, are less likely to show inappropriate aggression towards strange dogs.

Top: *The anal glands secrete substances which provide important information about the dog and its sexual and social status.*

AGGRESSION BETWEEN DOGS IN THE SAME HOUSEHOLD

Dogs living in the same household need to have a hierarchy – in other words, they need to establish an order of dominance. Problems often arise when a new puppy, introduced to a household with an older resident dog, reaches social maturity: any time from 18 months to two years of age (the teenage years!). At this age, it will begin to challenge the older dog. It may try to take over a preferred sleeping place or a favourite toy, for example. Fights will start if the older dog does not wish to give way.

It is important to decide which dog is likely to win in an aggressive encounter. If the older dog has become feeble and is unlikely to win the next few battles, you need to reinforce the younger dog's bid for dominance, even though you might feel that you are betraying an old friend in some way. You can do this by feeding it first, allowing it access to preferred areas, and giving it attention before the other dog. If the older dog is still strong, is of a larger breed and is most likely to win any battles, reinforce the older dog's status as just described.

There will be no peace in the household until this problem is sorted out. In situations where both dogs are reasonably equal, you may need to re-home one of them or they will be constantly fighting. Speak to your behaviourist.

Do not leave the two dogs alone together until the hierarchy has been established between them. Fights can be quite savage.

PREVENTING AGGRESSION BETWEEN DOGS IN THE SAME HOUSEHOLD

If you decide to have a second dog:

- select one that is of the opposite sex to your resident dog
- do not leave the two dogs alone together in confined spaces
- do not give food to groups of dogs.

Above: *Challenges may occur between dogs in the same household, usually in the form of body posture. You should back the dog most likely to win, or there will never be peace in the house.*

▶ BARKING ◀

Barking is probably the dog behaviour least well tolerated by people, especially in suburban areas. Some breeds bark more readily than others. Terriers, for example, bark at the slightest provocation, while Siberian Huskies rarely bark and Basenjis only yodel. It is a natural means of canine communication. In some instances, however, dogs begin to bark excessively and this becomes a serious problem.

There are many potential causes of frequent barking and it is important to establish the cause in each case. The tone and pattern of the barking may provide some clues as to the reason for it. The dog that begins barking as soon as its owner leaves the house, and continues to do so, usually in a monotone, throughout the owner's absence may be suffering from separation anxiety (see pp99–100).

Some dogs bark sporadically throughout the day. This is usually in response to some trigger stimulus such as the movements of neighbours or the presence of a neighbouring dog.

Some dogs bark excitedly for quite some time when their owners arrive home. This barking is a problem only if the neighbours are complaining; these dogs are not usually distressed. If, on the other hand, your dog is barking during your absence and the neighbours are complaining about the disturbance, try to enlist their help in correcting the problem. Ask them to note down the times at which the dog barks and also how long it barks. If the dog is barking continuously until you return, it may be suffering from separation anxiety. This is a serious behavioural problem and you will need the help of an animal behaviourist.

If the dog barks at the person who delivers the post, at passers-by in general, or when neighbours come and go, try leaving the dog inside with toys and a comfortable bed so that it is not so easily stimulated by these events. If you know that you will have to leave the dog for a while, make sure it has had a long run or a vigorous play session before you leave. It is much more likely to relax and sleep while you are out if it is tired.

Dogs that bark while their owners are at home can be trained to be quiet on command. Such dogs can also be 'desensitized' to triggers such as doorbells and postmen.

Above: *Puppies are capable of displaying inter-dog aggression, just like adult dogs.*

COMMON BEHAVIOUR PROBLEMS

PREVENTING PROBLEM BARKING

- Train your puppy to respond to a 'Quiet!' command (see p76, Training).
- Expose your puppy or new dog to as many unusual sights and sounds as possible, as frequently as possible and reward it for calm behaviour at this time.

- When your dog or puppy becomes over-excited and excessively vocal, redirect its behaviour by asking it to sit or lie down for a reward. Try to get it to concentrate on you and a food treat and ignore the stimulus that caused the barking.

▸ DESTRUCTIVE BEHAVIOUR ◂

Destructive behaviour is very much more common in young dogs. Puppies need to chew, especially during teething, as this soothes their aching or itching gums – it is also a way of exploring and investigating their worlds. Older dogs may also be destructive. This may be play related or, if it happens while the dog is left alone, may be due to separation anxiety (see pp99–100).

Puppies can be very destructive if not managed properly. If your puppy starts to chew furniture or doors, tell it 'no' firmly and give it one of its own toys to chew. Whenever you see it chewing its own toys, praise it. If the puppy persists, try using a water pistol. Squirt the puppy in the face when it starts to chew. Do not say anything. It is best that the puppy associate the unpleasant event with the object it is chewing, not with you.

Water pistols can work with older dogs too. Another option is to apply a deterrent such as bitter lime to objects that may be chewed.

PREVENTING DESTRUCTIVE BEHAVIOUR

- Train your young puppy to chew its own toys.
- Do not leave puppies or newly acquired older dogs alone where they are able to get access to valuable furniture.

Leave them in a laundry area with plenty of toys or maybe a bone to chew.

Top: *Destructive chewing is a nasty behavioural trait, and it can become obsessive.*

▶ DIGGING ◀

Dogs dig to bury a toy or a bone, to uncover something they can smell or that they know has been buried, to make a hole in which they can keep warm or cool off, or simply to play. Soil is fun because it moves and changes. They may also dig to escape under a fence.

Digging can cause problems where the dog is forever digging up recently planted or carefully nurtured gardens, or managing to escape by tunnelling under fences.

If a dog digs obsessively and cannot be distracted from the behaviour, it may be suffering from an obsessive-compulsive disorder (see pp100–1). This needs to be dealt with by an animal behaviourist.

If your dog is digging in unacceptable areas, redirect it to an area that is its own. This might be a sandpit or a waste area of the garden.

If the dog persists in digging in the unacceptable area, you could try burying inflated balloons in the region, or investing in snappy trainers, which are a little like plastic mousetraps. These snappy trainers are triggered by the digging and fly up with a snapping noise, which startles the dog.

Digging beneath fences can be successfully prevented by electrifying the fence with a suitable voltage. (Check that your local council will allow this.)

PREVENTING DIGGING
- Make sure your dog has plenty of interactive play every day, as well as lots of exercise.
- Redirect digging behaviour to another, more acceptable play.
- Give bones in a confined area where it is impossible for the dog to bury them.

▶ HOUSE SOILING ◀

This is most common in puppies while they are being house-trained. House soiling may also occur in older dogs for various reasons.

If an adult dog suddenly starts house soiling, take it for a complete health check, as there may be an underlying problem such as cystitis (bladder infection) or enteritis (bowel infection). If the dog is old, there could be a problem with control of bladder or bowel, or it may be due to senility.

Above: *Although it is perfectly normal for a dog to dig holes, its owners are less likely to approve, especially if they happen to be keen gardeners.*

If the dog is house soiling only when the owners are out, it may be suffering from separation anxiety (see pp99–100). This will require the help of an animal behaviourist. Other possible reasons include territorial marking and asserting dominance – or habit as in dogs adopted from kennels.

Extreme excitement and overly submissive responses to people often trigger urination. This sometimes happens when owners return home or visitors arrive. The dog is apparently unaware that urine is being passed. Most will outgrow the excitement trigger as they gain better bladder control, and it is best ignored. Submissive urination, however, does require treatment.

If a male dog is lifting his leg inside, he may be marking out a territory and trying to assert his dominance over one or more people or other dogs in the household. This is sometimes seen if a new family member arrives, or someone comes to stay.

Neutering can achieve a 75 per cent reduction in this behaviour. Retraining may also be necessary. The offender should be confined to certain parts of the house and should always be under direct supervision when indoors. If he shows signs of marking, he should be startled with a foghorn or water pistol and put outside.

As with puppy training, it is important to take these dogs outside frequently and praise them for elimination. Male adult dogs will rarely void all their urine at one time so a long walk helps to encourage them to fully empty their bladders. This should also help to decrease the likelihood of marking indoors. Dogs kept in groups indoors are most at risk for inappropriate elimination. Males and females may be stimulated to urine-mark, and may also defecate indoors. It is easier to keep groups of dogs in an outdoor compound with minimal house access.

Dogs that have been kennelled all their lives, and are adopted at the end of their breeding life, commonly soil inside. They have learned to eliminate on hard surfaces, and the floor is no different to the base of a run or a concrete yard. These dogs need retraining and this is often difficult as substrate preference (getting used to eliminating on grass or earth as opposed to hard surfaces or carpet) is learned at a very young age (seven to eight weeks). Retraining is done in the same way as training a new puppy.

Particularly submissive dogs may urinate spontaneously when anyone reaches towards them. This is a normal canine response to meeting with a dominant animal, but can become quite a problem. Some of these dogs will assume a submissive posture and urinate simply because someone looks directly at them.

It is possible to train these dogs by rewarding them for less submissive behaviour such as sitting and looking at their owners. Any rolling over or urinating should be ignored.

PREVENTING HOUSE SOILING

- Train young puppies thoroughly.
- Ensure adequate exercise and outdoor access especially for entire (non-neutered) males.
- M7ake the dog feel at ease with newcomers.
- Keep groups of dogs in outdoor compounds.

▶ SEPARATION ANXIETY ◀

Separation anxiety is a name used to describe the behaviour seen in some dogs when they are left alone, or when they are separated from one particular family member.

These dogs typically begin barking as soon as their owners leave and continue throughout their absence. They may chew doors, rip up carpet and curtains in the house, destroy furni-

abandoned or if they were abandoned because owners could not cope with the dog's separation anxiety.

These dogs are extremely anxious when left alone. They require specialist treatment which usually involves anti-anxiety medication and a behavioural modification programme. This is a series of exercises that the dogs and owners must perform daily to teach the dogs to relax and to stay relaxed while their owners leave the room, and eventually the house.

PREVENTING SEPARATION ANXIETY
- Make sure your puppy gets used to spending time alone.
- Try to avoid having the puppy spend time with one family member exclusively. Make sure it learns to feel comfortable with everyone in the household.
- Avoid establishing a departure ritual. Vary the order of shower and breakfast. Put on shoes and coat then sit down for a cup of coffee.
- Don't make an issue out of leaving and don't fuss too much when you return.
- Exercise your dog well before leaving it alone for any length of time.

ture and defecate and urinate inside. In extreme cases they have been known to jump through glass windows.

There may be an inherited predisposition to this condition. It is interesting that there is a high incidence of separation anxiety in dogs from rescue centres. It is unclear whether the condition is related to the trauma of being

▶ OBSESSIVE-COMPULSIVE DISORDER (OCD) ◀

This is usually a normal behavioural trait that is being performed with abnormal frequency, to the point that it interferes with daily living and becomes a nuisance. Examples of this behaviour include digging, chasing shadows, a dog chasing its tail, snapping at imaginary flies, running along fence lines and chewing at feet.

Dogs with OCD cannot usually be distracted from their behaviour. If they are enticed to stop, it is only for a short while. Some dogs may become aggressive towards anyone who tries to physically prevent the behaviour from continuing, while others will not even stop long enough to go for a walk or eat properly. In very severe cases, such animals may damage themselves physically. Compulsive diggers may dig until their feet bleed and their nails are broken.

Chewers and tail chasers may cause self-inflicted skin lesions and may then suffer secondary infections.

Top: *Your dog depends on you for comfort, companionship and food. Most dogs will learn to come to terms with their owner's absence during the day.*

Animals with obsessive compulsive disorder have a deficiency of certain neurochemicals in the brain, and need professional help. They require medication and behavioural modification designed to redirect their attention and to encourage relaxation. In many cases they need medication throughout life.

PREVENTING OCD

It seems that this condition may be inherited and is probably impossible to prevent this, so it is wise not to breed from affected animals. Genetically predisposed breeds include Scottish Terriers, Bull Terriers (tail chasing), and King Charles Spaniels (fly snapping).

▶ ESCAPING ◀

Some dogs insist on trying to escape and go exploring. This can be frustrating for owners and dangerous for the dogs. If you own an escape artist, the single most important consideration is perimeter fencing. Ensure that this is at least 2–3m (6–10ft) high, or if the dog is likely to dig its way out, bury part of the fence 1m (3ft) below the ground. You could also use a sonic barrier, which emits a pulse of high-frequency sound at regular intervals. Another option is to build a secure pen with a concrete floor and a roof, in which you can leave the dog while you are out or too busy to interact with it. It is important that your dog receives plenty of exercise and interactive play with you every day. If being involved in whatever you are doing stimulates your pet, it is less likely to wander off exploring. If your dog is well exercised it will probably be happy to relax and sleep while you are busy doing something boring, or if it has to stay home alone for a while.

Male dogs may run off after bitches in heat. Castration (see p44, De-sexing) will deal with this problem.

Above: *Although it looks comical when a dog chases its tail, this game may become an obsession, especially in dogs that are frequently lonely.*

PROTECTING YOUR DOG'S HEALTH

▶ THE VETERINARY CLINIC ◀

To keep fit and well your dog needs regular health care. Some of it will be provided by you, and some by your local veterinary clinic. Veterinary clinics are not just centres for the treatment of ill health. They are also a valuable source of practical information and friendly advice from veterinarians and their trained staff. Most veterinary clinics also act as valuable community resource centres, providing information about local boarding facilities, dog groomers or dog-sitting services, for example. Many also have notice boards on which their clients can post information.

The changes in veterinary science, and particularly during the last decade, have been remarkable. In addition to radiography (X-rays) and routine blood sampling, modern diagnostic aids include ultrasonography (ultrasound scanning equipment), Magnetic Resonance Imaging (MRI) and Computer Assisted Tomography (CAT) scans. Other areas of veterinary specialization include:

- Anaesthesia
- Orthopaedics
- Ophthalmology
- Endocrinology
- Dermatology
- Animal Behaviour
- Dentistry
- Medicine
- Surgery
- Radiology
- Diagnostic imaging

Certain methods of diagnosis and therapy – some ancient, some new – are also becoming a recognized part of a comprehensive approach to animal health care. Known as Complementary Veterinary Medicine (or Complementary and Alternative Medicine – CAVM), many of these methods have been used in human medicine for years, but their integration into veterinary practice has been comparatively recent. For example, some veterinarians are now trained in veterinary acupuncture and acutherapy (examination and stimulation of specific points on the body of animals using acupuncture needles, injections, low-level lasers, magnets, etc for diagnosis and treatment), veterinary chiropractic (examination, diagnosis and treatment through manipulation and adjustments of specific joints, particularly the vertebrae, and of the skull), veterinary massage therapy, homeopathy, botanical medicine, nutritional therapy and the use of flower essences.

Left: *Some dogs may develop a real fear of the veterinary clinic: if this happens, visit your clinic socially and ask your vet and clinic nurse to fuss over the dog and give it treats.*

The bodies of animals, like those of humans, have many defence mechanisms to protect them against the microorganisms in the environment. They work well when an animal is healthy, but are less effective if the dog is weakened, unhealthy or mentally or physically stressed.

PRIMARY BARRIERS

- Mucous membranes in the nose, trachea and bronchi help trap foreign substances and prevent them from entering lungs.
- The liver destroys toxins produced by bacteria.
- Healthy skin acts as a physical barrier.

- Acid in the stomach kills many invading organisms.
- Organisms are excreted in faeces and urine.
- Mucus produced from the lining of the intestines acts as a barrier.

Most organisms that cause disease consist mainly of proteins. If an organism gets past the primary barriers, the body quickly detects its 'foreign' proteins and produces antibodies against them. Antibodies are produced by specialized white blood cells found mainly in the lymph nodes and spleen. They circulate in the blood and are usually very specific, destroying only the organism (the antigen) that stimulated their production.

The first time the dog's body encounters a disease, introduced from the environment or by means of a vaccine, it may take up to 10 days to produce antibodies. The next time the disease is encountered, antibody production occurs rapidly, preventing the disease from becoming established.

Antibody levels wane with time, but if the antigen is encountered again (either through infection or a booster vaccination), antibody production immediately resumes. Immunity created by vaccines is not generally as long-lasting as the 'natural immunity' created by exposure to a disease. This explains why booster vaccinations may be needed to keep an animal protected.

PASSIVE (MATERNAL) IMMUNITY

Passive immunity occurs when a newborn animal acquires antibodies from its mother. Newborn animals have a rudimentary immune system that takes six to 12 weeks to fully develop. To tide them over this period they receive passive immunity from their mother in the form of antibodies, some of which enter their body while they are still in the uterus, but most of which are taken in with the mother's colostrum (first milk). This is a critical period for the newborn, as it can only absorb these antibodies during the first day or two after birth.

If a bitch has a prolonged whelping or gives birth to a large litter, the early puppies will have more opportunity to ingest colostrum than those born later, so the degree of passive

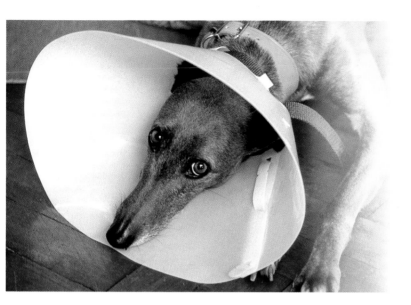

immunity may vary between littermates. A bitch can only pass on antibodies to the diseases that she herself has encountered, or against which she has been vaccinated.

A bitch that is not vaccinated, or lives in isolation from other dogs, will have fewer antibodies to pass on, and her puppies will be more vulnerable from birth. A bitch used for breeding must be vaccinated, and her booster vaccinations should be kept up to date.

Passive immunity is temporary: the amount of antibodies in the blood halve every seven days or so, and after three months it has almost disappeared.

ACTIVE IMMUNITY

Active immunity is the result of an animal producing antibodies from its own immune system, in response to disease or vaccination.

To be protected, puppies must develop their own, active immunity, by contact with a disease or through vaccination.

While passive immunity is high the puppy is protected from disease, and its own immune system may not respond to a vaccination. However, some brands of vaccine are designed to override passive immunity and stimulate the puppy's immune system.

Some puppies may lose passive immunity before three months, so these puppies will be at risk if they are not vaccinated and are exposed to a virus.

The typical recommendation for a puppy from a bitch that has been properly vaccinated is to receive two vaccinations, one at nine weeks of age and the other at three months. In areas of high risk, vaccination may be started at six weeks and repeated at fortnightly intervals until three months. Ask your veterinarian for advice about the situation in your area.

Top: *A simple Elizabethan collar, made from paper or sturdy plastic, will prevent a dog from scratching, licking or aggravating its wounds and causing secondary infection.*

▶ VACCINATING YOUR DOG ◀

While still with the breeder, some six-week-old puppies will have received a temporary vaccination against canine distemper, hepatitis and canine parvovirus (CPV). At nine weeks your puppy should be vaccinated against distemper, infectious canine hepatitis (ICH), CPV and 'kennel cough'. Depending on where you live, it may also need vaccinations for other diseases such as leptospirosis or rabies. A booster will be required three weeks later. Some brands of vaccine are effective against several diseases, which reduces the number of injections required. Your veterinarian will advise you which vaccines are the most suitable for your dog.

CANINE DISTEMPER

This is the first virus disease of dogs for which a vaccine was specifically developed. The distemper virus also affects ferrets, foxes, skinks, raccoons and wolves. Once a killer disease, it is now uncommon in many countries because of long-term routine vaccination programmes. Originally it was most often seen in young animals, although now adult dogs are likely to be affected. This is usually because their vaccinations have not been kept up to date.

Early symptoms include loss of appetite, and affected dogs develop a respiratory infection accompanied by a sore throat, coughing and fever and a thick yellow purulent discharge from the eyes and nose. There may be enteritis accompanied by diarrhoea.

The disease can progress over the next two to three weeks as the virus infects the nervous system, causing muscle tremors, seizures and even paralysis. Dogs that recover may be left with permanent damage to their nervous system. Those infected as puppies often show deformities of the enamel on their permanent teeth caused by damage while these were growing. Some dogs develop thickened pads, hence distemper's other name: 'hard pad' disease.

Top and opposite: *Vaccinations can be given either under the skin or as drops into the nostrils of a dog. Your veterinarian will advise you which type of vaccination is necessary for your pet.*

CANINE PARVOVIRUS (CPV) INFECTION

This disease is similar to feline enteritis in cats, and may have resulted from a mutation in that cat virus. It first appeared in the late 1970s and spread rapidly around the world. It is spread by dog-to-dog contact through the faeces, and the virus is easily carried from one place to another on the hair or feet of infected dogs, on contaminated cages and on human clothing or footwear. The virus can survive for long periods, and is resistant to extremes in environmental conditions. In very young puppies this disease causes inflammation of the heart muscle (myocarditis), often resulting in sudden death and a very high death rate among litters. Puppies that survive can take weeks to recover. In older puppies and adults it causes fever, enteritis (accompanied by diarrhoea and vomiting) and a death rate of up to 10 per cent.

INFECTIOUS CANINE HEPATITIS (ICH)

This virus infection occurs mainly in young dogs, is highly infectious and can cause serious liver damage. Many infected dogs show no symptoms, while others may simply appear 'off-colour' over a long period of time. In both cases these dogs excrete the virus in their urine and spread the infection amongst other dogs.

Symptoms can vary from a mild fever to a serious illness, followed by death within a few hours. Affected dogs lose their appetite, are very thirsty, have a discharge from the eyes and nose and may develop bloody diarrhoea. Early treatment of affected animals is essential if there is to be any hope of recovery. Some that survive develop opacity of the cornea of the eye, which makes it appear blue.

KENNEL COUGH

This mild, self-limiting disease can affect dogs at any age, and is caused by a combination of various infectious agents, including the bacterium *Bordetella bronchiseptica* and canine parainfluenza virus. Inflammation in the trachea and bronchi causes varying degrees of 'dry' cough, sometimes accompanied by retching or gagging.

Kennel cough is a highly contagious disease and is transmitted through moisture droplets coughed into the air by affected animals; this is why it spreads rapidly among dogs that are closely confined, such as in kennels (hence the name given to the disease), hospitals and pet stores. The peak time for infection is during the summer months when dogs are more likely to be brought together in boarding kennels. Kennel cough is more of a nuisance than a threat to life, but the dry cough can persist for up to three weeks, causing the dog (and its owner as well) a great deal of distress. Kennel cough often gets worse when the dog is excited.

Vaccines are available, which are given every three months by injection under the skin or by placing drops directly into the dog's nose.

Most boarding kennels will not accept dogs unless they have been recently vaccinated.

LEPTOSPIROSIS

In many countries, including the UK, this is another disease against which dogs should be routinely vaccinated. There are many different types (serovars) of *Leptospira* bacteria, all of which are spread through infected urine. The bacteria can also infect humans. Symptoms of infection depend on the serovar involved. For example, *Leptospira canicola* infects the kidneys and frequently results in chronic kidney disease. In mild cases the dog may merely appear 'off-colour' for a few days. In serious cases, signs include lethargy, bad breath (caused by uraemia, the accumulation of urea in the blood), ulceration in the mouth, and vomiting. In advanced cases there is severe abdominal pain. Treatment includes antibiotics and therapy to replace lost fluids. Recovered dogs have kidney damage that contributes to chronic kidney disease later in life.

Leptospira icterohaemorrhagiae, which is often caught from rats, infects the liver and causes substantial damage. In acute cases death can occur quickly. Signs to look out for in your dog include lethargy, vomiting, bloody diarrhoea and jaundice. Early treatment with antibiotics and fluid replacement is essential.

RABIES

In countries where this viral disease is endemic, dogs are routinely protected by vaccination. Rabies can affect any mammal and is almost always fatal. Transmitted through the saliva of infected animals, usually the result of a bite, it can also be spread by infected saliva coming into contact with mucous membranes (eye, nose or mouth) or a skin wound.

In Europe, foxes are the most important carriers of the infection. In North America, raccoons, bats, skunks, foxes and coyotes are the animals most commonly diagnosed with rabies, whereas in Mexico and other Latin and Central American countries, dogs are the most common carrier.

The incubation period can range from two weeks to six months. The virus travels via the nerves to the brain, where it causes inflammation (encephalitis) resulting in nervous symptoms. In the last stages of the disease the virus moves into the salivary glands and saliva.

In its early stages, rabies commonly causes behaviour and personality changes – for example, nocturnal animals are seen out during the day, wild animals may lose their fear of humans, and quiet animals may become excitable or even turn aggressive. Affected dogs tend to hide away from light.

As the disease progresses, about 25 per cent of affected dogs show the 'furious' form and are likely to attack other animals or humans without provocation. Animals affected by the 'furious' form of rabies are extremely dangerous to approach, so it is important to practise caution when doing so. Within six days of the appearance of their symptoms they usually enter a coma and die.

HUMAN HEALTH AND LEPTOSPIROSIS

Leptospirosis is only one of several dog diseases that can infect humans. Always be aware of the need for hygiene. Make sure all family members (especially children) wash their hands after handling a dog. If you need to handle a dog that may be infected with leptospirosis, wear rubber gloves.

The remainder develop the 'dumb' form, in which early paralysis of the throat and cheek muscles make it unable to swallow, so that saliva drools from the animal's mouth. These animals rarely survive more than two weeks, also becoming comatose before they die.

PREVENTION

In certain countries where rabies is endemic, the law requires the vaccination of dogs and cats. Many island nations in which the disease is not endemic (such as Hawaii, Australia and New Zealand) have strict quarantine laws to prevent its introduction. In Britain the PETS scheme allows vaccinated cats and dogs to enter under certain conditions.

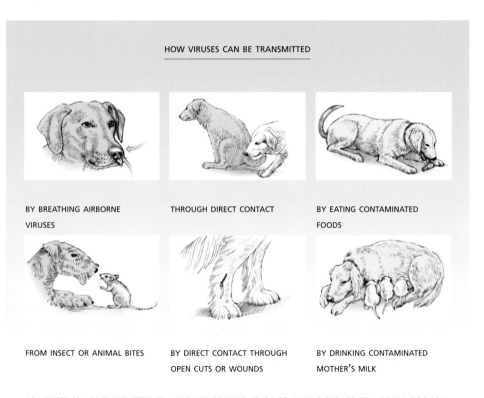

HOW VIRUSES CAN BE TRANSMITTED

BY BREATHING AIRBORNE VIRUSES

THROUGH DIRECT CONTACT

BY EATING CONTAMINATED FOODS

FROM INSECT OR ANIMAL BITES

BY DIRECT CONTACT THROUGH OPEN CUTS OR WOUNDS

BY DRINKING CONTAMINATED MOTHER'S MILK

AS VIRUSES CAN BE TRANSMITTED IN A NUMBER OF WAYS, IT IS NOT ALWAYS EASY TO TELL HOW A DOG MAY HAVE CONTRACTED A VIRAL DISEASE.

Top: *In this microscopic view of a dog's brain, the small red bodies inside the purple brain cells are indicative of a rabies infection.*

PRECAUTIONS

If your dog fights with any mammal that is a rabies carrier, saliva carrying the virus could be present on its coat or in any of its wounds.

- Do not try to capture the attacking animal.
- Take extreme care when handling your pet. Use gloves, and cover it with a towel.
- Allow as few people as possible to handle it.
- Call Animal Control or any other equivalent organization.
- Take your pet to a veterinarian.
- If your pet has a current rabies vaccination, get advice about giving a booster within 72 hours (this is compulsory in the United States).
- In the United States, if your pet does not receive a booster within 72 hours, then unless the attacking animal tests negative, your pet will be quarantined for six months at a veterinary clinic or disposed of by the local Animal Control.

If you are bitten or scratched by an animal suspected of being rabid, or if saliva from the animal enters an open wound or comes into contact with your nose, eyes or mouth, wash the wound or contact area with household detergent or soap. These kill the virus faster than any disinfectant.

It is essential that you then get medical attention immediately. The treatment involves a course of vaccinations.

ROUTINE RABIES PREVENTION

- Do not feed or attract wildlife into your garden.
- Call Animal Control if you suspect that there is a rabid animal in your yard.
- Do not allow bats to live in the attic or chimney of your house.
- Do not try to capture wildlife.
- Do not pick up dead or abandoned animals.
- If you think you are particularly at risk (if you regularly handle dead animals or their nervous tissue, or if you live within an endemic area), consult your physician about whether you should be vaccinated.

Above: *This stray, eight-week old mongrel puppy arrived in its new home with a severe case of roundworm. After six weeks and the correct treatment, it is altogether a different creature.*

▸ PARASITES ◂

Dogs may suffer from a variety of parasites, which are grouped into internal parasites and external parasites (those that live on or in the skin, such as fleas and mites). Most parasites are host-specific, which means that they infect one particular species of animal only. Among the exceptions, though, are the cat flea, cattle tick and sheep tick, which may also infect dogs.

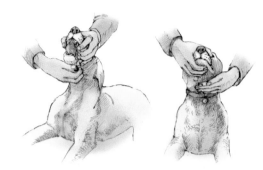

WORMS

A variety of worm species can infect dogs. These are classified according to their shape or the region of the body that they infect. Those of most importance in the dog – are roundworms, hookworms, whipworms, tapeworms, lungworms and heartworms.

ROUNDWORMS

The two most common species found in dogs, *Toxocara canis* and *Toxascaris leonina*, are ascarid worms.

Toxocara canis is particularly important because of its ability to infect puppies before they are born. An infected bitch has roundworm larvae lying dormant in her muscles and other tissues, and these are largely unaffected by many routine worm treatments. Hormones released during pregnancy stimulate these larvae to migrate; some move into the bitch's intestine and develop into adult worms, others migrate into her uterus and into the unborn puppies' lungs. At birth, more larvae are excreted in the bitch's milk.

The result is that almost every puppy is born with a roundworm infection, and all are likely to be infected as soon as they suckle. During the next few days and weeks they will also pick up infection by ingesting some of the roundworm eggs now being produced by adult worms in the bitch's intestine and passed out in her faeces. In an infected puppy the larvae migrate through the intestinal wall and, via the liver, to the lungs. If there is a large number of larvae, the puppy may cough and have breathing problems – it may even develop pneumonia.

From the lungs some larvae enter the bloodstream and are circulated to the muscles and other tissues, where they form cysts and lie dormant. Others are coughed up and swallowed. By the time the puppy is two weeks old these have developed into adult worms capable of laying thousands of eggs. Some adult worms may be clearly visible in the puppy's faeces – these then infect the bitch when she licks the puppy clean.

Puppies suffering from a heavy roundworm infestation have a harsh coat, fail to grow properly and suffer from diarrhoea and a bloated abdomen. If worms are present in large numbers they can block the stomach and intestines.

Top: *The correct way to administer tablets to a dog is to press its upper lips over its upper teeth and firmly force the muzzle open. Use your other hand to place the tablet as far back on the tongue as possible. Hold the muzzle closed and the head back until the tablet is swallowed.*

Toxocara canis can also have an 'indirect' life cycle, in which infective larvae lodge in the tissues of another animal (called a paratenic host), and only develop if that animal is eaten by a dog.

Infection with *Toxascaris leonina* is less of a problem because its larvae do not migrate through the lungs and body tissues, but complete their development within the walls of the bitch's intestine. Therefore puppies do not become infected with this particular roundworm.

TREATMENT

Assume that, to some degree, all nursing bitches and their puppies are infected with roundworms, so start treatment as soon as possible. Some vets recommend that a pregnant bitch be treated every two weeks; others suggest less often.

At the time of writing, there is no product that will remove all encysted or migrating roundworm larvae, so the treatment aims at destroying any developing adult worms in the intestine.

The first worm treatment for puppies is usually given when they are two to three weeks old, followed by further treatments every one to two weeks until they are three months old. Further worming should be given at monthly intervals until six months, and then three or four times a year for the rest of each dog's life.

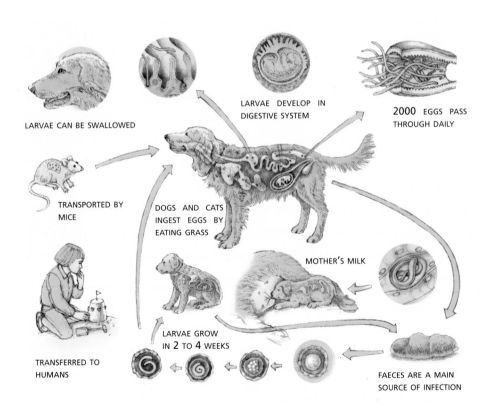

LARVAE CAN BE SWALLOWED

LARVAE DEVELOP IN DIGESTIVE SYSTEM

2000 EGGS PASS THROUGH DAILY

TRANSPORTED BY MICE

DOGS AND CATS INGEST EGGS BY EATING GRASS

MOTHER'S MILK

TRANSFERRED TO HUMANS

LARVAE GROW IN **2** TO **4** WEEKS

FAECES ARE A MAIN SOURCE OF INFECTION

THE LIFE CYCLE OF THE ROUNDWORM AND ITS INTERACTION WITH ITS HOSTS AND HUMANS

Your veterinary clinic will recommend products and a regime appropriate to your area.

Because of the hazard to human health, everyone, especially children, must thoroughly wash their hands after handling young puppies.

Properly dispose of faeces from a nursing bitch and her puppies. Burn them in the garden, or flush them down the toilet. Do not bury or compost them, because under the right conditions roundworm eggs can survive for years.

WORMS AND THE HUMAN

The eggs from roundworms and hookworms can infect humans. Puppies are often infected with worms, and children are especially at risk, particularly those at the thumb-sucking stage.

Dogs that are harbouring worms shed worm eggs in their faeces, and under the right conditions these can remain for years in grass or soil in home gardens and community parks.

When swallowed by a human, roundworm eggs hatch into infective larvae that do not develop into adult worms but wander through the body, causing damage. They are potentially dangerous because they move through internal body tissues (a process called visceral larva migrans). The disease is called toxocariasis, and it produces a variety of symptoms depending on which tissues are affected. Occasionally larvae become encysted in the retina at the back of the eye, causing partial loss of sight or even total blindness.

Proper hygiene is essential. Make sure that all members of the family wash their hands after handling or playing with a dog, and before they eat. Do not allow a dog to lick somebody's face, or to eat off crockery used by humans. If hookworms infect humans, the larvae enter and migrate through the skin,

leaving a visible raised, irregular track (a process called cutaneous larva migrans). The disease is self-limiting and a spontaneous cure occurs after several weeks.

Two dog tapeworms, the hydatid tapeworm (*Echinococcus granulosus*) and the flea tapeworm (*Dipylidium caninum*), can infect humans. The flea tapeworm rarely causes problems, but the hydatid tapeworm (which is not found in the UK) is potentially lethal, causing hydatid disease. Cysts develop in the liver and lungs, and less commonly the heart, kidneys and central nervous system, and death can result. Children are commonly infected, but because the cysts are slow growing it can be many years before the disease is recognized.

Dog and cat fleas (*Ctenocephalides canis* and *Ctenocephalides felis*) bite humans. Most people suffer minor irritation, but some are allergic to fleas and may develop a more serious skin reaction. Proper flea control will minimize the problem.

HOOKWORMS

These are small, round-bodied, blood-sucking worms that live in the dog's intestine and, if present in sufficiently large numbers, can cause severe anaemia and death.

The two species most commonly encountered in dogs are *Ancylostoma caninum* and *Uncinaria stenocephala*. In some areas another species, *A. braziliensis*, also occurs. The most common hookworm in tropical and subtropical regions is *A. caninum*, while in the United Kingdom, Europe, Canada and northern United States, *Uncinaria stenocephala* is more likely to be implicated.

Adult hookworms lay eggs that are passed out with the faeces and hatch into larvae on the ground. Under the right conditions (damp and humid soil) these can survive for many months. In places where dogs congregate and defecate, such as public parks where faeces have not been removed, or grass runs in breeding or boarding kennels with poor hygiene, large numbers of infective larvae can build up.

Dogs become infected either by swallowing larvae or by penetration of larvae through the skin; the most common site of penetration is between the toes, and this often causes itching and dermatitis. Larvae eventually reach the dog's intestine and develop into adult worms to complete the cycle. Hookworm larvae can also penetrate human skin.

Ancylostoma caninum larvae can infect puppies via the bitch's milk in a similar way to *Toxacara canis*. When any dog becomes infected, some larvae migrate through body tissues and become encysted in the muscles, where they lie dormant. In a bitch, hormonal changes in late pregnancy stimulate the encysted larvae to migrate into her mammary glands. They are then ingested by the puppies when they drink the colostrum, and later the milk.

The symptoms of hookworm infection include poor growth in puppies or loss of condition in adult dogs, diarrhoea and anaemia. Treatment is the same as for roundworms.

WHIPWORMS

Trichuris vulpis has a 'direct' life cycle in which eggs laid by adult worms in the intestine are passed out in the faeces and hatch out into infective larvae that are then capable of infecting a dog and growing into adult worms.

Symptoms of whipworm infection include failure to gain weight or loss of condition, diarrhoea and, in severe infestations, anaemia.

TAPEWORMS

Tapeworms have an 'indirect' life cycle in which another animal (called the intermediate host) must eat the worm eggs before the larvae inside them can develop any further.

When a dog eats the intermediate host, the life cycle is completed and the adult worm develops. Several species of tapeworm can infect dogs: *Taenia taeniaeformis*, *Taenia pisiformis*, *Taenia hydatigena* and *Taenia ovis*.

Above: *The whipworm hatches from its egg, within the dog's body.*

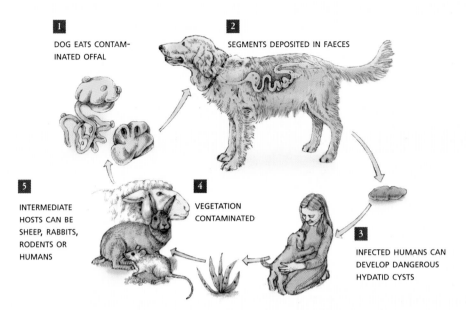

1 DOG EATS CONTAM-
INATED OFFAL

2 SEGMENTS DEPOSITED IN FAECES

3 INFECTED HUMANS CAN
DEVELOP DANGEROUS
HYDATID CYSTS

4 VEGETATION
CONTAMINATED

5 INTERMEDIATE
HOSTS CAN BE
SHEEP, RABBITS,
RODENTS OR
HUMANS

THE LIFE CYCLE OF THE HYDATID TAPEWORM

Although some of these worms can grow to up to 3m (10ft) long, they usually cause few health problems and often go unnoticed.

One of the more common tapeworms is *Dipylidium caninum*, often called the 'flea tapeworm' because fleas act as the intermediate host. One of the first signs of tapeworm infection is the presence of tapeworm segments sticking to the hair around a dog's anus, lying on its bedding or in its faeces. Initially these resemble cucumber seeds, but when dry they look more like grains of rice.

From the time your puppy is three months old, treat it monthly against tapeworms and roundworms until it is six months old. Thereafter, worm every three months throughout your dog's life. Many worm preparations are only effective against particular parasites, so ask your veterinarian which to use. Proper flea control will help to reduce the incidence of *Dipylidium. caninum*.

The hydatid tapeworm, *Echinococcus granulosus*, is not found in the UK, but is particularly serious because it poses a risk to human health.

The worm itself is only about 7mm (0.2in) long, but an infected dog may harbour more than a thousand. Eggs passed out in the dog's faeces are eaten by a variety of intermediate hosts, among which are sheep and humans. Inside the intermediate host, the eggs develop into larvae that form cysts in the tissues, especially the liver and lungs.

Working dogs on farms, especially sheep farms, are the most at risk because they may have access to raw offal containing the cysts.

In some countries where *Echinococcus* infection was proving a problem, for example Wales and New Zealand, national control schemes were introduced that prohibited the feeding of raw offal to dogs and ensured that all working dogs were wormed regularly.

LUNGWORMS

Lungworms (*Filaroides osleri*) also have a 'direct' life cycle. Adult worms develop in small (2mm; 0.8in) nodules in an infected dog's trachea and bronchi. They lay eggs that are coughed up, and either swallowed and passed out in the faeces, or transmitted through the dog's saliva. A mild infection of lungworms in a dog may go unnoticed. In more severe infections, though, symptoms include weight loss and a protracted, harsh cough, especially during even moderate exercise.

Treatment of lungworms can sometimes prove difficult, although today there are several different drugs available. Ask your vet for advice.

HEARTWORMS

The heartworm (*Dirofilaria immitis*) infection is spread directly from dog to dog by certain species of biting mosquito. Heartworm larvae (called microfilariae) circulate in the blood of an infected dog. When a mosquito sucks blood from that dog it also ingests the microfilariae, transferring them to other dogs that it bites. After the microfilariae enter the bloodstream, they travel in the circulation to the heart, lungs and large blood vessels, where they eventually mature into adults that begin to produce the next generation. After being bitten by an infected mosquito it may be six to seven months before microfilariae can be detected in a dog's blood, so heartworm disease is not often confirmed in dogs under a year old.

In the early stages of heartworm infection a dog will show few symptoms, but these develop later as large numbers of parasites become established and cause damage to the lining of the heart and obstruct the heart and blood circulation of the animal.

An affected dog gradually loses weight, becomes lethargic and starts to tire easily. It may develop a persistent cough and become anaemic and pot-bellied. Eventually it may suffer right-sided heart failure.

If you live in an area where heartworm disease occurs, your dog may need regular blood tests to determine whether it is infected. Talk to your veterinarian about this.

Tests include microscopic examination of a blood sample from your dog to detect the microfilariae, using a special stain to make them more visible. At least half of all infected dogs have no circulating microfilariae, so you may find that other tests are needed to help confirm the presence of the disease.

Uninfected dogs can be given a course of drugs to prevent infection, and infected dogs can be treated. Treatment sometimes results in severe side effects because dead worms disintegrate in the bloodstream and cause blockages in some blood vessels.

PROTOZOAN INFECTIONS

TOXOPLASMOSIS

Toxoplasmosis, caused by the protozoan parasite *Toxoplasma gondii*, is common in cats and can be spread to humans from the ingestion of the cysts passed out in cat faeces. Toxoplasma infections in dogs are uncommon and most go unnoticed, but be aware that a dog that eats cat faeces can become infected and may suffer similar symptoms to infected humans.

HOW HUMANS CAN BECOME INFECTED

• handling contaminated cat litter or garden soil in which cats have defecated
• accidentally ingesting contaminated soil on unwashed fruit or vegetables
• eating raw or undercooked meat (especially sheep meat)
• consuming unpasteurized goat's milk, yoghurt or cheese.

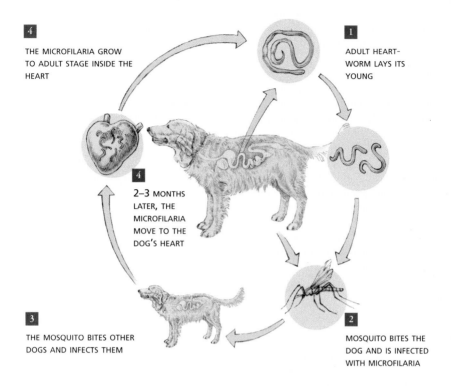

4 THE MICROFILARIA GROW TO ADULT STAGE INSIDE THE HEART

1 ADULT HEART-WORM LAYS ITS YOUNG

4 2–3 MONTHS LATER, THE MICROFILARIA MOVE TO THE DOG'S HEART

3 THE MOSQUITO BITES OTHER DOGS AND INFECTS THEM

2 MOSQUITO BITES THE DOG AND IS INFECTED WITH MICROFILARIA

THE LIFE CYCLE OF THE HEART WORM

One in two humans have a chance of becoming infected at some stage of their life. Initial infection may pass unnoticed or cause little more than 'flu-like' symptoms.

However, the parasite may become encysted in various tissues, causing inflammation, and toxoplasmosis is especially dangerous to pregnant women, in whom it may cause abortion or infect the baby in the womb. An infected baby may be born blind or retarded.

As a routine precaution, cat faeces should be removed from a litter tray every two days, before any of the toxoplasma eggs in them become infective.

COCCIDIOSIS

Although uncommon, four species of coccidia (*Cystoisospora*) can infect dogs. Young puppies are most at risk, and symptoms include diarrhoea, dehydration and weight loss. Diagnosis is by laboratory examination of faecal samples. Veterinary treatment is essential.

GIARDIASIS

The protozoan parasite *Giardia lamblia* occurs worldwide and can infect humans, most domestic animals and birds. Adults (trophozoites) mainly inhabit the mucosal surfaces of the small intestine, where they interfere with digestion. They produce cysts that are passed out in the faeces. These cysts often end up in water, which then becomes a source of infection. In pet animals, giardiasis is principally a problem of dogs, but cats are occasionally infected. Signs vary from mild to severe diarrhoea that may be persistent, intermittent or self-limiting. Some animals experience weight loss, others do not.

The disease is diagnosed by laboratory examination of faecal samples. There are several drugs that may be used for veterinary treatment of giardiasis.

FLEAS

As soon as you get your puppy, treat it for fleas, even though it may not appear to be infested. Your vet will advise you about the best available treatments for these external parasites, which will need repeating throughout your dog's life. If you have a cat, make sure that you treat it as well, because the cat flea is the most common flea species found on dogs.

Permitted to go unchecked, fleas can transmit internal parasites; dogs eating adult fleas can become infected with the tapeworm *Dipylidium caninum*. Fleas themselves can also be carriers for diseases such as bubonic plague and endemic typhus.

The adult female flea feeds for two to three days, consuming up to 15 times her own body weight of blood every day, then begins to lay eggs. At peak production a female can lay up to 50 eggs a day, and many hundreds of eggs in her lifetime. The eggs are not attached, and normally drop off onto the floor, carpet, animal's bedding or ground.

The eggs hatch out into legless larvae that find their way into cracks where they feed on organic debris. This includes flakes of skin and the faeces of

Above: *Unfortunately, a far-too familiar sight: a dog scratching frantically at its fleas. It's not enough to treat only your dog – treat all your other household animals and your home.*

of fleas on dogs and cats in 12 hours. Applied to the skin, they spread over the skin surface and kill adults on contact. They also kill 99 per cent of flea larvae in the pet's immediate surroundings. The effects of such treatments last for about a month.

It is not enough just to treat your dog, though; you must treat any cats in the household, and treat the home environment as well.

adult fleas (which contain incompletely digested blood). After four to eight days the larvae spin a protective cocoon and form pupae.

These flea pupae can remain dormant for up to two years and are particularly resistant to some of the most commonly used insecticides.

The flea pupae hatch when the environmental conditions are right – the hotter and more humid, the better. Hatching is triggered by the warmth or vibrations of a potential host (dog, cat or human), and can take less than a second. Newly hatched fleas can leap about half a metre (20in), about 1200 times their own body length, and move onto a host to feed. Under ideal conditions the complete cycle can take as little as three weeks.

Fleas spend quite a lot of time off the host and in the environment, so treatment must aim at two things:

- killing adult fleas on the dog and in the surroundings
- breaking the life cycle by killing eggs and larvae in the surroundings.

TREATING THE ANIMAL

Treating a dog for fleas will kill the adults on it and the few eggs that may remain in the dog's coat. There are many effective treatments available, some of which kill 95–100 per cent

TREATING THE ENVIRONMENT

Because fleas spend only a short part of their life cycle on a dog, it is important to treat the immediate environment in which the adult fleas live, and where their eggs develop.

Regular vacuuming of carpets and special attention to crevices in wooden floors and along skirting boards will help to physically remove many of them, but it also concentrates larvae inside the vacuum bag, together with plenty of organic matter for them to continue feeding. If the bag is disposable, remove and burn it. If not, put a flea collar into it to kill the inhabitants.

Flea 'bombs' or 'foggers' are available to treat the home. These release an insecticidal mist containing permethrin, which kills adult

Top: *The adult flea, laying an egg. At peak production she could lay up to 50 eggs a day. The eggs drop off onto the carpet or the dog's bedding – or your bedding, if you're not careful.*

fleas, and methoprene, an insect growth regulator based on a natural compound found in insects that prevents the development of flea larvae. It remains in the carpet for up to nine months and prevents the development of flea eggs and larvae.

For the most effective results you should treat the whole house. Each of the rooms to be treated must be vacated and closed off, and any fish or house plants should be removed.

Once you have prepared the house, let off the bomb and close the rooms for at least two hours. Next, open the doors and windows to ensure that the rooms are properly ventilated before people and animals are allowed to re-enter, 30 minutes later. If you use one of these products, follow the instructions on the label. Some carpet shampoos contain insecticides that will kill fleas, and regular use of these may help control the problem.

FLEA-BITE DERMATITIS

Many dogs (and cats) develop an allergy to flea saliva. In temperate climates it is often called 'summer eczema', and even one flea bite can trigger off a severe reaction that has the dog scratching and biting itself, causing damage to its skin. In many cases, veterinary treatment is essential, because the allergic reaction must be controlled. Any severe skin damage needs to be treated to prevent bacterial infection and promote healing.

TICKS

Ticks mainly infest farm livestock, particularly sheep and cattle, and certain wild animals. In temperate climates they are more active during the summer months. They can also cling onto dogs' hair, insert their mouth parts through the skin and suck blood. Once their abdomen is engorged to about the size of a pea, they drop off again. They can then survive for up to two years without another feed.

If you live in a tick-infested area, or have taken your dog for a walk through countryside where sheep or cattle have been grazing, thoroughly check your dog's skin to locate and remove any ticks. Pay special attention to the inside of your dog's ears, head, neck and shoulders, between its forelegs and under its belly. Keep in mind, however, that once engorged with blood, some ticks drop off again. In some cases all that is visible is a rash around the bite site.

When removing a tick, try to extract the head, otherwise an abscess may form. This removal is not always easy to accomplish.

You could spray the tick with a flea spray, leave it for 12 hours, then remove the dead tick.

For a quicker result, though, you could dab some methylated spirits or alcohol onto the tick to relax or kill it, wait a few minutes, then use a pair of fine-pointed tweezers to grip the tick near its head and pull it out with a sharp jerk. Do not grip it by the body, though, because squeezing it could result in the injection of more saliva, which might contain toxin (see tick paralysis).

If an abscess forms at the site, bathe it in warm saline and use an antibacterial ointment recommended by your vet.

Inset: *When you remove a tick from your dog, try to extract the head – which can be a problem – otherwise an abscess may form on your dog's skin.*

TICK PARALYSIS

Many ticks generally cause temporary discomfort, but in warm coastal areas of Australia there is an Ixodes species whose saliva contains a toxin that can cause gradual paralysis and even death. Symptoms of tick paralysis develop about four to five days after infestation.

Initially, affected dogs show weakness in the hindquarters. This extends forwards, and there may be some change in the tone of the bark and some difficulty in breathing. Eventually paralysis may lead to death from respiratory failure. Veterinary treatment is essential.

LICE

These are uncommon, and are usually found on neglected dogs. There are several types, of which the most common is the biting louse (*Trichodectes canis*), which chews on flakes of skin and causes mild irritation. A more severe irritation is caused by the common sucking louse (*Linognathus setosus*), which penetrates the skin to feed on tissue fluids and blood, and can cause anaemia.

Louse eggs (nits) can be seen attached to hairs of the dog. The tiny grey-white adult lice, about 2mm (0.08in) long, can be seen particularly around the ears, head, neck, shoulders and anus.

Because lice spend the whole of their life cycle on their host, treatment is easy and consists of insecticide sprays or washes given

at five- to seven-day intervals for at least three treatments. Infected bedding should be destroyed and the area disinfected.

EAR MITES

There are several species of mite that can infect dogs. Ear mites (*Otodectes cynotis*) usually cause most problems for puppies, but they do also infect adult dogs and cats. They cause irritation that leads to the dog scratching and the introduction of a secondary bacterial infection that causes inflammation and pain. Diagnosis is by microscopic examination of a swab taken from the ear. Uncomplicated cases of ear mite infection may be treated with insecticidal ear drops (if you own a cat, you will need to treat it as well). If secondary infection is present, though, antibiotic treatment (with drops and/or by injection) will be necessary.

Above: *The correct way to restrain a dog is to place it on a firm surface, put one arm gently around its neck and the other under its abdomen. Use both arms to hold the dog firmly.*

MANGE MITES

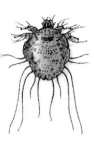

Three species of mange mite most commonly infect dogs. *Cheyletiella yasguri* lives among the hairs and on the skin surface and causes scaling (dandruff) and irritation, which may lead to hair loss and skin infection.

The sarcoptic mange mite (*Sarcoptes scabei*) and the demodectic mange mite (*Demodex canis*) can cause severe problems in dogs.

Demodectic mites enter the hair follicles, causing hair loss and mild irritation.

Sarcoptic mites burrow into the skin and cause severe irritation, which sets the animal rubbing, scratching and biting. Symptoms include itchiness and the appearance of bare patches where hair has been rubbed off or fallen out. Veterinary diagnosis is by microscopic examination of skin scrapings.

Treatment of *Cheyletiella* infestation is fairly simple, using an insecticide lotion or cream. Treatment of sarcoptic or demodectic mange is more difficult and prolonged because the mites burrow deep within the skin.

TIE A SOFT BANDAGE AROUND THE MUZZLE.

TAKE THE CLOTH AROUND THE NECK AND TIE AT THE BACK.

TEMPORARY MUZZLES CAN BE MADE FROM SOFT BELTS, TIES OR EVEN OLD TIGHTS

HARVEST MITES (CHIGGERS)

These small mites (*Trombicula autumnalis*) occur in some areas, As their name implies, they are most common in late summer/early autumn, during or after harvest time. The adult mites are free-living, but their small red larvae are parasitic. In dogs these larvae, which are just visible to the naked eye, most commonly infect the feet between the toes (the interdigital space) and the small pocket at the lower edge of the ear flap. They cause irritation, and affected dogs constantly rub their ears and/or lick their feet. If your dog becomes infected, consult your veterinarian as he or she can recommend a suitable treatment.

Inset: *A species of mange mite that infects dogs. Similiarly with other parasites, it is best to treat the dog as soon as the mites are detected.*

A BASIC FIRST-AID KIT

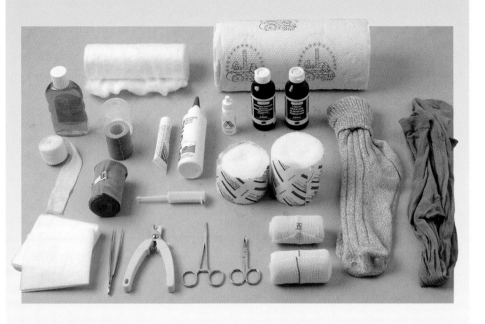

The information given here is for guidance only, and is not intended to replace veterinary advice. If faced with an emergency, remember that the principles of first aid for dogs are similar to those for humans.

- Rolls of 5cm (2in) and 7.5cm (3in) bandage
- Self-adhesive bandage
- Roll of 5cm (2in) crepe bandage
- Roll of 5cm (2in) and 7.5 (3in) wide adhesive plaster
- Non-stick gauze pads
- Cotton wool balls
- Tweezers
- Curved, blunt-ended scissors
- Straight scissors
- Length of strong, soft bandage or tape to use as an emergency muzzle (see p122)
- Nail clipper

- Antiseptic and disinfectant liquids recommended by your vet
- Tube of antiseptic cream
- Hydrogen peroxide (three per cent) for flushing wounds
- Mineral oil for treatment of constipation
- Ear and eye drops as recommended by your vet
- Roll of absorbent paper towel
- Leg from old pair of pantyhose (to put over the head if ears are bleeding)
- Old sock (to protect a dressing on the lower limb)

MONITORING YOUR DOG'S HEALTH

The earlier you can detect a health problem in your dog and do something about it, the better. Treatment is more likely to be effective, and your dog will probably suffer less discomfort or pain. Learn what is normal, so you can detect when something abnormal occurs. Whenever in doubt, though, call your veterinary clinic.

▶ EARLY SIGNS OF ILL HEALTH ◀

One of the first signs of ill health may be a subtle change in your dog's normal behaviour. It may be quieter than usual, less active, or disinclined to go for a walk. It may be thirstier, or less hungry. Since dogs, like humans, have their 'off' days, you should keep an eye on this sort of change for a day or two. If it continues, then take further action.

Consult your veterinarian if your dog shows any of the following signs:

- unusual tiredness or lethargy
- abnormal discharges from body openings
- excessive head shaking
- markedly increased or decreased appetite
- excessive water consumption
- marked weight loss or weight gain
- abnormal behaviour such as aggression, lethargy or hyperactivity
- abnormal swellings on any part of the body
- excessive scratching, licking or biting at any part of the body
- lameness
- difficult, abnormal or uncontrolled waste elimination
- difficulty in getting up or down.

As soon as you see anything unusual, make a note of it, for you may need this information if you take your dog to a veterinarian at a later date. While doctors can talk to their human patients for a 'history', veterinarians will have to rely on the pet owner in this case!

Left: *If you suspect that your dog may be ill, take it to a vet for a thorough examination.*

▸ PAIN ◂

Pain results from the stimulation of specialized nerve endings (receptors) in the body. It has many causes, but is usually the result of injury, infection, poisoning, or inflammatory reaction. It is one of the earliest signs of disease.

If we suffer pain, we are able to tell someone. A dog cannot speak, but there are ways in which it can demonstrate how it feels. Some dogs, particularly those of the smaller breeds, react to the slightest incident, while others, especially the hounds, are rather more stoical. However, in most cases your dog's reactions will be fairly clear.

It will usually yelp in pain if you accidentally step on its foot or something has struck it. It may cry out if you touch a very painful part of its body, and may even snap at you. However, sometimes the only indication that something is wrong may be a less obvious change in your dog's behaviour.

- If it has hurt a leg it may put the foot of the affected leg on the ground but place no weight on it, limp, or carry the leg off the ground.
- If the dog is suffering from joint pain, for example from arthritis, it may cry out when getting up or lying down.
- Cramp will cause muscle tremors, and the dog may whimper.
- Pain or irritation from its anal glands will cause it to 'scoot' its bottom along the ground. The dog may turn and frequently inspect the painful hind-end.

- Pain in an eye will cause it to paw at the affected area or rub it against objects.
- Pain in an ear usually results in the dog tilting its head to the affected side, and shaking it frequently.
- Mouth pain may cause salivation, and the dog may yawn frequently.
- It can be more difficult to detect when a dog is suffering spinal, head or internal pain.

Above: *A vet checks for joint and spinal pain in this young mongrel.*
Opposite: *Use a round-ended pair of scissors to trim excess hair, so as not to hurt the dog.*

SUSPECT SPINAL PAIN IF YOUR DOG:

- seems to be lame, but no limb is affected
- resents being touched along its back
- humps its back and/or trembles when standing up
- is incontinent
- has difficulty assuming normal posture for defecation
- collapses on its hindquarters.

SUSPECT HEAD PAIN IF YOUR DOG:

- has half-closed eyes, but there is no obvious eye problem
- presses the top of its head against objects
- gently but regularly shakes its head
- stares vacantly.

SUSPECT INTERNAL PAIN IF YOUR DOG:

- spends more time lying down, and/or lies in a curled-up position
- is particularly restless, and unable to settle down
- keeps its abdominal muscles tensed or stands in a hunched-up position
- adopts a 'prayer' position, with forelegs down and hind legs up
- continually looks around at its abdomen, or bites or licks at it
- continually strains to pass a bowel movement, but fails
- is usually submissive and easily managed, but inexplicably becomes aggressive.

WHAT TO DO

If the pain was caused by a minor accident (for example if someone stepped on the dog's toe), use common sense and monitor the outcome. If pain persists after a few hours, contact your local veterinarian.

If you can't determine the cause or if pain is the result of something more serious, you will have to seek veterinary advise.

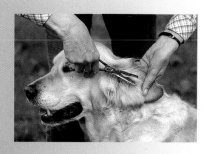

CLEANING YOUR DOG'S EARS

All dogs have some hair at the entrance to their ears, so regularly pluck out any excess hairs with your fingers (not too deep). Use round-ended scissors to trim away excess hair inside the ear flap.

Dogs sometimes scratch at one or both ears because they contain accumulated wax. This excess of wax can be due to hair blocking the ear canal, or a response to a minor irritation. If the ears are not inflamed or painful you can clean them yourself.

Use an ear-cleaning solution recommended by your vet. Twice daily, gently flood the ear canal with the fluid, massage externally, then wipe away excessive fluid and wax using cotton wool balls. Do not use any form of powder, or push anything down into the ear canal.

If the dog is still shaking its head after four to five days of this treatment, or if there is inflammation or pain, see your vet.

Above: *A veterinarian is able to detect ill health by looking at the eyes of this 12-week-old Border Collie.*

EAR PROBLEMS

SIGNS	POSSIBLE CAUSES	ACTION
Shaking head, black material in ear canal	Excessive wax accumulation	Clean ear(s) as on p127
Shaking head, scratching ears, gritty blackish discharge	Ear mites	Take to the vet to confirm (see p121–2, Ear mites)
Shaking head, reddish or yellowish-white, smelly discharge. Ear canal and inside of ear flap may be inflamed. Ear painful to touch	External ear infection (*otitis externa*). This is usually caused by a mixture of bacteria, fungi and yeasts. If left untreated it can cause severe pain and discomfort and lead to permanent ear damage	Do not place anything into the ear because the ear drum may be ruptured and some treatments may be harmful if they enter the middle ear. Take the dog to the vet, who will check that the ear drum (tympanic membrane) is intact, and may take a swab for culture to determine which infective organisms are present. Follow prescribed treatment

SIGNS	POSSIBLE CAUSES	ACTION
Shaking head, rubbing head on carpet, no obvious discharge, dog distressed, head held on one side	Foreign body in the ear canal, commonly a grass seed	Take the dog to the vet, who will remove the foreign body. Do not feed the dog prior to the appointment, as it may need a sedative
Head tilted to one side, loss of balance, abnormal movement of eyeballs (nystagmus). Dog may be vomiting	Middle- and inner-ear disease (*otitis media* and *otitis interna*). Can result from a foreign body or chronic ear infection	Take to the vet. Once the cause has been established, treatment may involve anti-inflammatory drugs, antibiotics and drugs (anti-emetics) to stop any vomiting
	Old dog vestibular syndrome. The cause is uncertain; it occurs suddenly in older dogs and responds to anti-inflammatory drugs.	Take to the vet
Swelling of the ear flap. Affected ear may be tilted downwards, and the head shaken	Aural haematoma. This is a build-up of blood or fluid between the cartilage and the skin of the ear flap. The cause is uncertain, but may be due to the dog shaking its head or scratching at the ear flap. It may also be the result of an auto-immune reaction	Wait 48 hours to allow time for the fluid to have finished accumulating, then take the dog to your vet. The vet may treat the condition medically or surgically. Treatment will involve draining the fluid and replacing it with antibiotics and anti-inflammatory drugs. With surgical treatment, under general anaesthetic, the area is opened and drained, then stitched to prevent fluid build-up
Superficial scabs on white ears; reddened skin	Sunburn	Purchase paediatric sunblock from your chemist and apply it to the affected areas three times daily. Try to keep the dog in the shade during the hours of most intense sunlight

SIGNS	POSSIBLE CAUSES	ACTION
Deep, long-standing scabs that have never healed	Cancer of the ear (squamous cell carcinoma)	Take to the vet. Treatment may involve cryosurgery (freezing with liquid nitrogen) or surgical removal of the pinna (ear flap)
Dog appears deaf	Wax blocking ear canal Inner ear infection (*otitis media*, *otitis interna*) Congenital defect Old age	Get a veterinary check to establish precise cause

MOUTH AND OESOPHAGUS PROBLEMS

SIGNS	POSSIBLE CAUSES	ACTION
Bad breath	Tartar build-up on teeth	Take to the vet. It will probably need to have its teeth scaled and polished
Bad breath, inflamed, bleeding gums	Gingivitis (inflammation of gums)	As above. Antibiotics may be necessary
Difficulty in eating, bad breath	Broken or infected tooth	Take to the vet. The tooth will need extraction; antibiotics may be needed
As above, may be bleeding, drooling tongue may be displaced	Tumour in the mouth (e.g. melanoma)	Take to the vet for assessment
Visible swelling under tongue	Ranula (blocked salivary duct)	Take to the vet
Drooling, pawing at mouth, may be gulping	Foreign body (eg bone or stick) lodged across the hard palate between upper molar teeth, or fish hook in lip	Open the mouth and check. If a foreign body is present and you can remove it, do so. Take care not to get bitten. If damage has occurred, or you can't find the cause of the problem, take the dog to the vet

SIGNS	POSSIBLE CAUSES	ACTION
Drooling, pawing at mouth, may be gulping	Bee sting in mouth (on tongue, inside cheeks or gum)	If you can see the sting, try to remove it with tweezers. Check the mouth regularly, and if more than slight swelling occurs, take the dog to the vet
	Ulcerated tongue	Check the tongue. If inflamed or ulcerated, investigate access to irritant or corrosive poisons. Take a sample of the suspected substance to the vet. See pp60–1, Poisons
Drooling, retching or coughing	Object stuck in the throat Kennel cough	Take to the vet in both instances
Regurgitating food, may be retching and salivating	Object stuck in the oesophagus Inflamed oesophagus	Take to the vet in both instances
Difficulty in eating, no other signs	Nerve problem	Take to the vet for diagnosis

STOMACH PROBLEMS

SIGNS	POSSIBLE CAUSES	ACTION
Eating grass, then vomiting grass and mucus (and bone)	Natural evacuation of indigestible material	Carry out protocol for vomiting in both instances (see p61, Emergency treatment)
As above, no bone	Mild gastritis	
Vomiting frequently, refusing food, depressed	Gastritis Pancreatitis	Take to the vet Take to the vet URGENTLY
As above, plus other possible signs including diarrhoea (with or without blood), dark tarry faeces	Bacterial infection from rotting or infected food Canine parvovirus infection Gastric ulceration Poisoning	Take to the vet in all instances

SIGNS	POSSIBLE CAUSES	ACTION
As above, plus hunched posture	Foreign body lodged in stomach Pancreatitis	Take to the vet Take to the vet URGENTLY
Distended abdomen, young dog, may be lethargic, poor coat	Worm burden	Treat for worms (see pp111–6)
Distended abdomen, retching, laboured breathing	Gastric dilation or torsion. The stomach has become filled with gas after eating or overeating, and may then have twisted round, blocking off the routes of entry and exit. More commonly seen in deep-chested breeds, e.g. Boxer, German Shepherd and Weimaraner, especially if the dog is exercised too soon after eating	URGENT ACTION REQUIRED Get veterinary help immediately Surgery may be needed

ASSESSING AND TREATING VOMITING

In dogs, vomiting is a natural way of eliminating material from the stomach, and does not necessarily indicate a problem.

If your dog vomits once or twice but otherwise appears bright, offer water only and monitor for four hours. If no more vomiting occurs, offer a small amount of bland food (such as cooked chicken and rice). If all is well, feed the bland food over the next 24 hours, then gradually reintroduce its normal diet.

Consult your vet if you are in any doubt, or if:

• the dog appears depressed

• there is blood in the vomit

• the dog is vomiting intermittently (e.g. every three to four hours) for more than eight hours

• the dog is vomiting continuously and cannot keep water down

• the dog has had access to household rubbish or poisonous substances.

SIGNS	POSSIBLE CAUSES	ACTION
Eating well but remaining thin	Worm burden	Treat for worms (see pp113–8)
As above, passing large amounts of pale faeces, may be eating own faeces	Exocrine pancreatic insufficiency	Take to the vet
Salivating or drooling, no other symptoms Salivation with weight loss, faeces appear normal or could have diarrhoea, vomiting	Inflammatory bowel disease. Several causes, which result in inflammation of the bowel and a reduction in its ability to absorb nutrients. May also be an associated bacterial overgrowth (abnormally high proliferation of certain bacteria).	Take to the vet
Eating excessively, may be eating unusual things	Exocrine pancreatic insufficiency. Malabsorption syndrome (inability to absorb nutrients properly) Anaemia	Take to the vet in all instances
Flatulence	Usually dietary, but also associated with old age. More common in certain breeds	Feed a highly digestible, low-fibre, moderately low-protein, soy-free, wheat-free diet
Chronic weight loss despite normal or increased appetite	Worms Tumour in bowel Malabsorption syndrome	Take to the vet to confirm cause
As above, intermittent vomiting and/or diarrhoea	Inflammatory bowel disease (see above)	Take to the vet
As above, but large amounts of grey or putty-coloured faeces	Exocrine pancreatic insufficiency	Take to the vet

SIGNS	POSSIBLE CAUSES	ACTION
Vomiting, not eating	Inflammatory bowel disease (see above) Foreign body Severe constipation	Take to the vet in all instances
Hunched-up posture	Abdominal pain Severe constipation	Take to the vet in both instances
Straining to defecate, hard firm faeces, straining ceases after passage of faeces, not vomiting	Mild constipation, particularly common in elderly dogs	Give mineral oil (1 teaspoon to 1 tablespoon, depending on dog size). If faeces are not passed within eight hours, take to the vet.
Constantly straining to defecate, few or no faeces produced, depressed, possibly vomiting	Severe constipation Prostate swelling preventing passage of faeces	Take to the vet to ascertain cause
Continuous straining, swelling at side of anus	Perineal hernia	Take to the vet. Surgical treatment is needed
Pain during defecation, 'scooting' bottom along floor, looking at and/or licking rear end. May be a discharge of pus	Anal gland impaction, inflammation or abscess	Take to the vet for treatment, which may include flushing out the affected gland(s) and treatment with antibiotics
Fresh blood in faeces	Colitis (inflammation of colon) Tumour Anal gland abscess	Take to the vet in all instances
Diarrhoea, one or two bouts, without blood, dog otherwise bright and alert, no vomiting	Food intolerance Mild bacterial enteritis	Offer water only for one day, then bland diet for 24 hours. If diarrhoea stops, gradually re-introduce normal diet. If diarrhoea continues, see your vet
Diarrhoea (intermittent), may be roundworms in faeces	Roundworm infestation	Treat for roundworms (see pp111–3)

SIGNS	POSSIBLE CAUSES	ACTION
Diarrhoea (frequent and persistent), dog otherwise bright	Giardiasis (*Giardia* infection) Coccidiosis	Take to the vet in both instances
Diarrhoea (frequent, may be blood), dog depressed and may have abdominal pain	Enteritis: bacterial (e.g. *Leptospira haemorrhagiae*) or viral (e.g. Canine Parvovirus, Canine Distemper, Infectious Canine Hepatitis. See pp106–7) Inflammatory bowel disease (see above) Malabsorption syndrome (inability to absorb nutrients) Colitis Tumour	Take to the vet in all instances

ENDOCRINE PROBLEMS

SIGNS	POSSIBLE CAUSES	ACTION
Abdominal enlargement, excessive thirst, symmetrical hair loss, pigment changes	Hyperadrenocorticism or Cushing's syndrome (excessive hormone production from adrenal gland)	Take to the vet
Lethargy, off food, may be vomiting, weight loss, middle-aged female	Hypoadrenocorticism or Addison's disease (inadequate hormone production from adrenal gland)	Take to the vet
Young dog, poor growth Older dog, lethargy, obesity, intolerant of cold, poor hair growth	Hypothyroidism (lack of thyroid hormone)	Take to the vet
Neck swelling, hyperactive, increased appetite, excessive thirst, increased urine output, panting	Hyperthyroidism (excess of thyroid hormone)	Take to the vet

SIGNS	POSSIBLE CAUSES	ACTION
Avoiding light, blinking	Several	Take to the vet
Runny eyes, clear discharge	Wind, dust, strong sunlight, allergy or blocked tear duct. Some dogs may be born without a tear duct	Bathe with cooled, boiled water or ophthalmic saline. If it doesn't clear in a few days, take to the vet
As above, sudden onset, eyelids swollen, may be rubbing at face Runny eyes, clear discharge, inflamed conjunctiva	Urticaria (acute allergy to sting or other allergen) Hair rubbing on eye (trichiasis or districhiasis) Entropion (in-turned eyelid)	Take to the vet in all instances
As above, dog coughing Runny eyes, clear or purulent discharge, bottom lid appears to be gaping, conjunctiva very inflamed Runny eyes, purulent discharge, whites of eyes inflamed, pawing at eyes As above, hair loss around eyes As above, one eye only	Kennel cough Ectropion (out-turned eyelid) Bacterial or viral conjunctivitis Canine Distemper Infectious Canine Hepatitis Demodex infection Possible foreign body in eye, or injury to eye	Take to the vet in all instances

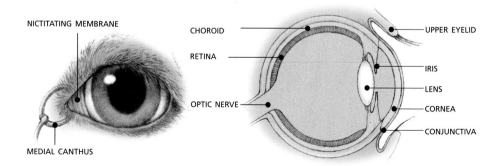

NICTITATING MEMBRANE

MEDIAL CANTHUS

CHOROID

RETINA

OPTIC NERVE

UPPER EYELID

IRIS

LENS

CORNEA

CONJUNCTIVA

Above: *Although similar to the human eye, the dog has a higher number of light-sensitive cells as well as a nictitating membrane.*

SIGNS	POSSIBLE CAUSES	ACTION
Tacky, purulent discharge. Eyes seem dry. Conjunctiva inflamed	Dry eye (keratoconjunctivitis sicca)	Take to the vet
Growth of tissue over cornea, may appear brownish	Pannus	Take to the vet
Eyes appear white, dog's vision appears to be affected	Cataract formation	Take to the vet
Dog appears to be going blind, but no other symptoms	Retinal degeneration Progressive Retinal Atrophy (inherited) Collie Eye Anomaly (congenital)	Take to the vet in all instances
Reddish lump in corner of eye, young dog. Common in Bulldogs	'Cherry eye'. Excessive tissue growth on third eyelid	This will need surgery. Take to your vet
Area of skin with hair growing out of it, on conjunctiva and/or cornea and lids	Ocular dermoid (growth)	Take to the vet. This requires surgery
Small growth on upper or lower eyelid	Periocular granuloma	May need surgery. Take to the vet
Dog closing one eye, may be avoiding light, apparent pain, eye watering	Inflammation within the eye (uveitis)	Take to the vet
As above, white line or dot on the surface of the eye, pain, eye watering	Corneal ulcer. Often the result of a cat scratch	Take to the vet
Third eyelid showing	Nerve damage	Take to the vet
Pressing head against objects (sign of headache), eye appears protruding, avoids light	Glaucoma (swelling of the eyeball due to accumulation of fluid causing increased pressure)	Take to the vet

LIVER, SPLEEN OR PANCREATIC PROBLEMS

SIGNS	POSSIBLE CAUSES	ACTION
Abdominal distension, with or without jaundice	Liver tumour	Take to the vet
Abdominal distension, excessive thirst, pale gums, lethargy	Tumour of spleen causing internal bleeding	Take to the vet
Vomiting, jaundiced, dark urine, may be abdominal pain, poor appetite	Bile duct blockage (bile stones, bile sludging, inflammation, infection) Bile duct rupture	Take to the vet in both instances
Vomiting, diarrhoea, jaundice, blood in urine	Leptospirosis (see p108)	Take to the vet
Off-colour, lethargic, fever, bloody diarrhoea	Infectious Canine Hepatitis (see p107)	Take to the vet
Acute, persistent vomiting, fever, abdominal pain	Pancreatitis. Pancreatic digestive enzymes may be secreted into the pancreatic tissue itself, causing severe inflammation and tissue destruction. Can cause widespread damage and death. Recovered animals may suffer permanent dysfunction of the gland	Take to the vet
Dry scaly coat; weight loss; large quantities of light-coloured, soft, smelly faeces; coprophagia (eating own faeces)	Exocrine Pancreatic Insufficiency (EPI). Some or all of the part of the pancreas that secretes digestive enzymes is missing. Digestion of fats, particularly, is difficult, and faeces contain large amounts of water and undigested fat. Fatty acid deficiency causes a dry, scaly coat. EPI is usually congenital, but may become apparent later in life (prevalent in German Shepherd Dogs)	Consult your vet, who will test a faeces sample from the dog. The usual treatment is enzymes, mainly trypsin, in tablet or powder form, and adjust the diet to include extra vitamin supplements and highly digestible oils (safflower or coconut)

LIVER, SPLEEN OR PANCREATIC PROBLEMS (CONTINUED)

SIGNS	POSSIBLE CAUSES	ACTION
Excessive thirst, hunger, may be abdominal enlargement, lethargy, weight loss	Diabetes mellitus. If the pancreas does not produce enough insulin, the result is diabetes mellitus. Glucose levels build up in the bloodstream (especially after meals). This results in glucose passing through the kidneys and into the urine, taking water with it. Breeds prone to diabetes include the Dachshund, King Charles Spaniel, Poodle (all types) and Scottish Terrier	Take your dog for a thorough check-up, including blood and urine tests. Mild cases may be controlled by adjusting the diet. In most cases diabetes mellitus can be controlled only by regular injections of insulin. These can be given at home
		Hypoglycaemic coma may occur in a dog receiving insulin injections if it is subject to excessive activity or exercise or goes for a long time between feeds. Inadequate glucose levels in the bloodstream are further lowered by the action of the injected insulin, leading to collapse, coma and convulsions. Treatment: give glucose or honey by mouth (always keep these substances on hand in case of an emergency)

NERVOUS SYSTEM PROBLEMS

SIGNS	POSSIBLE CAUSES	ACTION
Loss of balance, lack of coordination	Middle-ear infection Vestibular disease (infection, inflammation or tumour affecting the vestibule) Brain tumour Disease of cerebellum	Take to the vet in all instances
Seizures or convulsions	Epilepsy (more common in dogs up to three years old) Poisoning (see pp60–1) Brain tumour	Take to the vet in all instances

SIGNS	POSSIBLE CAUSES	ACTION
Fits, convulsions, head pressing, head pain	Inflammatory reaction of brain (encephalitis) Inflammatory reaction of brain lining (meningitis)	URGENT ACTION NEEDED Take to the vet
Collapsing, third eyelids visible, limbs rigid, tail straight, face contracting	Tetanus infection	Take to the vet
Salivating, may be other signs Salivating, behavioural change	Poisoning (see pp60–1) Rabies (see pp109–10)	Take to the vet
Abnormal head position (e.g. tilt), eyes may be flicking from side to side	Middle ear disease Vestibular disease (infection, inflammation or tumour affecting the vestibule) Brain tumour	Take to the vet
As above, old dog	Old dog vestibular syndrome (disease affecting the vestibule)	Take to the vet
Wobbling gait, scuffing feet, unsteady on feet especially after exercise (common in Bassets, Doberman, Great Dane)	Wobbler syndrome (cervical spondylopathy). Due to mal-formation of one or more cervical vertebrae causing bruising to spinal cord in neck	Treatment may be successful if caught early, otherwise prognosis very poor
Reluctant to move head, acute pain in neck	Cervical disc protrusion	Take to the vet
Collapsing in hindquar-ters, with or without acute pain	Disc protrusion in thoracic or lumbar region	Take to the vet
Weakness or collapse after exercise	Myasthenia gravis (neuro-muscular disorder)	Take to the vet
Sudden collapse, walk-ing in circles, partial paralysis, eyelids partly closed, eyes flickering	Stroke	Take to the vet

WHAT TO DO IF YOUR DOG IS LAME

You may be able to deal with some causes of lameness, but most will require veterinary attention. If you wish, you can use the following protocol to help you detect what area of a limb may be affected and get an idea of what the problem may be.

If the cause is not obvious, you can gently check the affected limb for signs of injury. First inspect the pads for an injury such as a cut or an embedded thorn. If nothing is visible, gently press each pad in turn to detect any painful area. Then, beginning at the toes, gradually work up the leg. As you do so, apply gentle pressure with your fingers and check your dog's response. When you reach an injured area your dog will probably react because the pressure is causing pain. To detect joint pain, gently manipulate each joint in turn.

If you are in any doubt as to what the cause is, or what to do, contact your vet.

SKELETAL, JOINT AND MUSCLE PROBLEMS

SIGNS	POSSIBLE CAUSES	ACTION
Slight lameness on one limb, one joint mildly painful when flexed or extended	Sprain (slight damage to ligament or cartilage in a joint)	Apply a cold compress, then use a crepe bandage to support limb. A severe sprain can lead to arthritis, so if it doesn't improve within 24 hours or if you are in doubt, get veterinary advice
Lameness hours after exercise, can bear weight on the foot of the affected leg	Muscle strain	Rest for two days. Gentle massage may help. If no improvement, take to the vet
Sudden lameness, cries if foot touched, toenail may be bleeding	Torn toenail	Take to the vet for trimming and antibiotics
Sudden lameness, reluctant to walk on hard surface, recent prolonged exercise on roads	Skinned pads	Exercise only on soft surfaces
Apply lanolin to affected areas
Use a spray to harden the pad

SIGNS	POSSIBLE CAUSES	ACTION
Sudden lameness, bleeding foot	Cut pad	If superficial, bathe in saline solution or cetrimide solution (1:20 dilution). Keep off hard surfaces for two weeks. If deep, take to the vet for stitching
Sudden lameness or acute pain during or after vigorous exercise, muscle tremors, unwilling to move, may also be crying	Myositis. Inflammation of the muscles with severe pain, swelling and difficulty in moving. Commonly occurs as cramp, caused by build-up of lactic acid in muscles after strenuous exercise and rapid cooling down (e.g. by jumping into cold water). Sometimes affects hind-leg muscles of Greyhounds during racing	Massage the affected limb and keep the dog warm. If pain persists, consult a vet
Similar to above, in Scottish or Cairn Terrier. Dog takes short, jerky steps. May involve the muscles of the forelegs and neck, with the dog unable to move	Scotty Cramp	Let the dog rest. The condition usually subsides after a few minutes. Discuss with your vet
Muscles on each side of the jaw swollen, mouth held open, dog in pain, eats with difficulty	Eosinophilic myositis. German Shepherds are particularly susceptible. Affects jaw muscles involved in eating. Onset is usually abrupt. Attacks last one to three weeks, time between attacks varies from three weeks to six months. Attacks become less severe but more frequent; after each attack the affected muscles become more atrophied	Get veterinary advice. It is a painful and progressive disease for which no cure has been found, although painkillers and anti-inflammatory drugs can help reduce the severity of an attack

SIGNS	POSSIBLE CAUSES	ACTION
Sudden lameness on one hind leg after vigorous exercise, touching toe to ground but not bearing weight on it	Ruptured anterior cruciate ligament in knee joint. A comparatively common injury that usually occurs as the result of an accident, such as slipping. Some dogs are more likely to sustain this injury because of the shape of their bones	Take to the vet, as surgery will probably be needed
Sudden lameness, holding one hind leg off the ground, yelping	Slipped knee cap (patella)	Take to the vet
Sudden lameness, hind limb twisted and painful	Hip dislocation	Take to the vet
Sudden lameness after fall or accident, swelling, pain, may be yelping	Bone fracture	Take to the vet
Sudden lameness, swelling of leg tissue	Bite wound	Take to the vet. The wound may be forming an abscess
'Bunny-hopping' gait, young animal	Hip dysplasia. Can be congenital or inherited. The head of the femur does not fit properly into the socket (acetabulum), so abnormal wear occurs in the joint, resulting in degeneration. German Shepherds and Labradors are more prone, and in many countries breeding dogs are screened for hip dysplasia in an attempt to eliminate the disease.	Take to the vet. This is a painful condition that cannot be cured other than by surgery
Sudden hind limb collapse, dog usually in pain	Intervertebral disc protrusion in thoracic or lumbar region	Request a house call. Or slide the dog onto a board and restrict movement, then take to the vet
Difficulty getting up or down, activity eases stiffness	Arthritis (degenerative joint disease)	Take to the vet

SIGNS	POSSIBLE CAUSES	ACTION
Difficulty in assuming normal posture for urination	Spondylosis (degenerative condition resulting in deposition of extra bone between vertebrae)	Take to the vet
Difficulty getting up and down, depressed, doesn't improve with exercise, off food	Spondylitis (infection of bone in one or more vertebrae) Bone cancer, usually spread from prostate cancer	Take to the vet Take to the vet
Swelling of one or more joints, dog depressed, sometimes off food, lame and lethargic	Arthritis (infectious or immune-mediated)	Take to the vet
Firm, painful swelling just above a joint, becoming larger over time; large dog	Bone cancer Osteomyelitis (bone infection)	Take to the vet Take to the vet
Acute forelimb lameness, neck pain, reluctant to move head	Cervical (neck) disc protrusion	Take to the vet
Chronic lameness affecting front leg in large breeds (e.g. German Shepherd or Labrador Retriever)	Elbow dysplasia (inherited condition) Arthritis (degenerative joint disease)	Take to the vet

SOME COMMON SKIN PROBLEMS

SIGNS	POSSIBLE CAUSES	ACTION
Scaly skin, white flakes within the coat	*Cheyletiella* (mite) infection (see p122)	Ask vet for an insecticidal treatment
Scurfy skin, particularly around head and shoulders, may be itchy. Tiny, greyish-white insects visible	Lice (see p121)	As above

SIGNS	POSSIBLE CAUSES	ACTION
Hair loss, symmetrical, no irritation, no broken hairs	Hormonal imbalance	Get veterinary advice
Bald areas, not symmetrical, no irritation, no broken hairs	Prolonged or excessive moult Dietary (fatty acid) deficiency	Take to the vet
Hair loss, not symmetrical, broken hairs visible, dog may react with a scratch reflex when its skin is rubbed	Self-inflicted through scratching, probably in response to an allergen	Take to the vet to determine the cause
Hair loss around eyes and possibly other parts of body. May be itchy. Pustules may be present	Demodectic mange	Take to the vet
Hair loss over a raised, pinkish area of skin. Not itchy	Ringworm (fungal infection)	Take to the vet
Scratching, skin reddened, oily, smelly and scaly	Yeast infection	Take to the vet
Scratching, excessive licking	Allergy to fleas, food, or something in the environment	If your flea control is adequate, take to the vet. If it isn't, treat for fleas (see pp118–20)
Scratching, chewing feet, late summer	Harvest mites (*Trombicula autumnalis*)	Ask vet for an insecticidal treatment
Scratching, chewing, hair loss on elbow region and feet	Mange (*Sarcoptes scabei*)	Take to the vet
Scratching, excessive licking, skin rash on underside of abdomen and inner thighs	Contact allergy Flea allergy	Take to the vet

SIGNS	POSSIBLE CAUSES	ACTION
Scratching, chewing, area inflamed and with pus, may be bleeding	Pyoderma (deep bacterial infection)	Take to the vet
Lump or swelling within the skin. Not painful	Lipoma (fatty tumour) Haematoma (blood blister) Skin tumour Sebaceous cyst	Take to the vet in each instance
Lump or swelling within the skin. Painful. May be discharging fluid	Abscess	Take to the vet
Persistent skin lesions around lips and feet, not itchy	Auto-immune condition	Take to the vet

SOME SIGNS OF URINARY PROBLEMS

SIGNS	POSSIBLE CAUSES	ACTION
Vomiting, abdominal pain, bad breath, straining, blood in urine	Acute kidney disease (nephritis)	URGENT ACTION REQUIRED. Get to the vet immediately
Excessive thirst, bad breath, dog may be passing large quantities of urine, may be mouth ulcers, weight loss, anaemia	Chronic kidney disease (nephritis) resulting from an infection, chronic degeneration, tumour or inherited defect	Measure and note the dog's water intake over a course of a day. Collect a sample of urine in a clean container, and take this with you to the vet for analysis.
Young dog, failing to thrive, excessive thirst, very pale urine	Juvenile renal disease (inherited)	Collect a sample of urine. Take sample and dog to the vet
Strong-smelling urine, with or without blood, frequent urination or leaking, may lick vulva or penis	Cystitis (inflammation of bladder) due to infection or bladder stones	Collect a sample of urine as above. Take sample and dog to the vet

SIGNS	POSSIBLE CAUSES	ACTION
Urine leaking from vulva or penis (urinary incontinence) As above, male dog As above, old dog	Sphincter incompetence due to hormonal or nerve problem Prostate problem Old age	Take to the vet in each instance
Male dog, straining to pass urine, may be vomiting	Urethral blockage, possibly by a bladder stone	URGENT ACTION REQUIRED. Take to the vet immediately

SOME SIGNS OF BLOOD AND CIRCULATORY SYSTEM PROBLEMS

SIGNS	POSSIBLE CAUSES	ACTION
Exercise intolerance and/or lethargy, weakness, possibly fainting. Puppy or young dog As above, any age As above, any age	Congenital malformation allows shunting of blood within the heart but by-passing the lungs (patent ductus arteriosus) Heart valve defect. Blood flows back through a valve, causing a heart murmur Anaemia	Take to the vet in each instance
Coughing	Congestive heart failure (chronic heart disease) Heart-based tumour Heartworm disease (see p116)	Take to the vet in each instance
Abnormal breathing	Anaemia Lung congestion due to malfunctioning heart Warfarin poisoning	Take to the vet in each instance
Pale or bluish tinge to gums	Malfunctioning heart Haemolytic anaemia (abnormal destruction of red blood cells) Warfarin poisoning Blood clotting disorder	Take to the vet in each instance

LABOURED BREATHING

If breathing is laboured, and/or there is abdominal movement associated with it, take the dog to a vet immediately.

THIS IS AN EMERGENCY

SOME SIGNS OF BLOOD AND CIRCULATORY SYSTEM PROBLEMS

SIGNS	POSSIBLE CAUSES	ACTION
Jaundice (yellow tinge to gums and whites of eyes)	Haemolytic anaemia (abnormal destruction of red blood cells) Secondary liver infection	Take to the vet in each instance
Abdominal distension	Fluid accumulation due to malfunctioning heart	Take to the vet

RESPIRATORY SYSTEM PROBLEMS

SIGNS	POSSIBLE CAUSES	ACTION
Sneezing, clear nasal discharge	Viral infection, allergy (e.g. to pollen), grass seed or blade of grass lodged in nose or a tumour	If persistent, take the dog to the vet
Sneezing, purulent nasal discharge from one or both nostrils	Bacterial or fungal infection Molar abscess	Take to the vet
Dry crusty nose Red, puffy skin on nose, with some crusting	Zinc deficiency Allergy (e.g. to pollen) Sunburn Allergy (e.g. to pollen)	Take to the vet If nose is red and sore, keep out of the sun. Apply paediatric sunblock. If problem does not subside, take to the vet
Noisy breathing, short-nosed breed (especially Cavalier King Charles Spaniel)	Elongated soft palate – a congenital defect. The floppy palate partly obstructs the larynx, interferes with respiration, and causes snorting while breathing.	Take to the vet for assessment
Noisy breathing, any breed. May be change in tone of the bark	Laryngeal problem (e.g. laryngitis)	Take to the vet
Choking, collapse, short-nosed breed	Elongated soft palate causing complete obstruction to breathing	URGENT ACTION REQUIRED. Open the mouth, extend head and neck, pull out tongue and gently press the chest to get the dog breathing

SIGNS	POSSIBLE CAUSES	ACTION
Choking, collapse, any breed	Foreign body in throat obstructing breathing	Try to remove the obstruction. Get urgent veterinary help
Rapid breathing	Pneumonia Heart problem Allergic asthma Poisoning (e.g. aspirin) Worm larvae migrating through the lungs	Take to the vet
As above, gums pale or white	Internal or external haemorrhage Poisoning (e.g. warfarin)	URGENT ACTION. Take to the vet
Abdominal movement associated with breathing	Diaphragmatic hernia (rupture of diaphragm after trauma) Pneumothorax (air in the chest, usually after trauma) Haemothorax (blood in chest) after anticoagulant (rat poison) poisoning Rib/lung damage after trauma	Take to the vet in each instance
Bleeding from nose	Acute trauma	Initially, place an ice pack (a packet of frozen vegetables) on the top of the nose. If bleeding continues, take to the vet
	Foreign body in nose Problem with clotting mechanism Poisoning with rodenticide (e.g. warfarin) Tumour	Take to the vet in each instance
Mild, occasional coughing	Tracheitis, allergy or a heart problem	Take to the vet
Frequent shallow coughing, has had a recent accident	Pneumothorax (air in chest)	Take to the vet
Coughing (frequent), honking	Tracheal collapse	Take to the vet. Usually treated by surgery

SIGNS	POSSIBLE CAUSES	ACTION
Frequent coughing, progressing to retching, white foam produced	Kennel cough or a foreign body in throat	Take to the vet
Frequent coughing, harsh, associated purulent nasal discharge, dog appears ill	Canine distemper	Take to the vet

STAGES AND DURATION OF OESTRUS CYCLE

PRO-OESTRUS	OESTRUS	MET-OESTRUS	ANOESTRUS
Vulva swollen with blood-stained discharge Bitch attractive to dogs but will not allow mating	Vulva very enlarged,discharge more straw-coloured. Bitch will allow mating. Ovulation occurs about two days after onset of oestrus	Occurs in unmated bitch. No external signs. Hormone changes equivalent to pregnancy. Around six to eight weeks after the end of oestrus a bitch may show signs of pyometra (see below) Around eight to nine weeks after the end of oestrus a bitch may show signs of false pregnancy	Sexual inactivity
Variable length. Average nine days	Variable length. Average nine days	Variable length. Average 90 days	Variable length. Average 90 days

SOME SIGNS OF REPRODUCTIVE PROBLEMS IN THE BITCH

SIGNS	POSSIBLE CAUSES	ACTION
Milky discharge from vulva, young puppy	Puppy vaginitis (mild inflammation of the vagina)	Usually self-curative. If in doubt, talk to your vet
Persistent thin, light-red discharge from vulva after oestrous cycle	Ovarian cyst	Take to the vet

SOME SIGNS OF REPRODUCTIVE PROBLEMS IN THE BITCH

SIGNS	POSSIBLE CAUSES	ACTION
Excessive thirst, reduced appetite, vomiting, distended abdomen, vulval discharge, six to eight weeks after oestrous cycle	Pyometra (fluid accumulation in uterus). Cause may be a hormonal imbalance	URGENT ACTION. Take to vet. May need surgical removal of uterus and ovaries
Enlarged mammary gland, not painful Enlarged mammary gland, painful, inflamed	Mammary tumour. Not always malignant Mastitis	Take to the vet in each instance
Milk production without pregnancy, bitch may be 'nesting' and protecting toys, may pant and/or appear nervous	False pregnancy (pseudo-pregnancy). Occurs in about 60% of non-neutered bitches. After one false pregnancy, she is likely to have one after each oestrous cycle	Distract bitch with increased exercise and play. Remove toys. If persists after about three weeks, contact vet. May need hormone treatment
Lethargy, loss of appetite, within a week or two of whelping. May be purulent discharge from the vulva	Metritis (inflammation of uterus)	Take to the vet. May need antibiotics, or bitch may need to be spayed

REPRODUCTIVE PROBLEMS IN THE MALE

SIGNS	POSSIBLE CAUSES	ACTION
Purulent discharge from penile sheath	Balanoposthitis (bacterial infection of sheath)	Clean the area daily with cooled boiled water and cotton wool. If discharge persists after five days, may need antibiotics
Enlarged testicle. May have symmetrical hair loss	Testicular tumour	Take to the vet for assessment
Spurting urination, blood in urine, straining to defecate	Prostate problem (tumour, abscess, enlargement), common in old dogs	Take to the vet for assessment

GROWING OLD

▶ A HAPPY RETIREMENT ◀

Like humans, dogs are living longer as the result of better nutrition and health care. Expected life spans vary between breeds, but compared to 20 years ago the life expectancy of pet dogs has increased.

There are now more elderly dogs in the canine population needing special care. And with increasing old age comes a gradual deterioration in health. While nothing can be done to stop the body's ageing processes, it is still possible to minimize their effects.

▶ SIGNS OF OLD AGE ◀

GREY HAIRS AND COAT CHANGES

One of the first signs of old age may be greying around the muzzle and eyebrows; however, this can occur in dogs as young as five years old, so it is not particularly significant.

During old age the coat tends to grow longer, even in short-coated breeds. The nails grow more quickly, too, so nail trimming is required more frequently.

DEEP SLEEP

Another sign is increasingly deeper and more prolonged sleep. Old dogs are more likely to be startled if woken suddenly, and some may even growl or snap at you if suddenly woken by being touched.

- You can help your elderly dog by giving it a bed in a quiet, peaceful corner where it can relax in comfort.
- Other pets should be kept away from it as much as possible.

CHANGES IN FEEDING AND DRINKING PATTERNS

- Loss of appetite, reluctance to eat or difficulty in eating. The latter may be an indication of gum inflammation (gingivitis) and/or it could be tooth decay.
- Increasing thirst. This may be a sign of developing kidney disease or it could be another health problem (see p125, Monitoring your dog's health).

Old dogs may benefit from a diet adjustment, so that the food is more easily digested and contains lower protein levels to lessen any stress on their weakening kidneys. Special therapeutic diets are available from your veterinarian, who may advise more frequent health checks and routine blood samples to monitor kidney and liver function (see pp124–51).

Left: *If you are tolerant and sympathetic towards your elderly dog's changing needs, it will enjoy a happy and comfortable old age.*

DIGESTIVE PROBLEMS

Symptoms include vomiting, diarrhoea and constipation. Important changes to the diet may include:
• three to four small meals daily (as for puppies)
• cooked eggs (this is the most easily digested protein)
• a prescription diet recommended by your veterinarian.

ARTHRITIC CHANGES AND OSTEO-ARTHRITIS

Old dogs, and those that have been left to sleep on hard surfaces or out in cold conditions for long periods, are more likely to show this condition. An early sign is stiffness when getting up and first moving around, which then improves. In more extreme cases the dog has difficulty in walking, weakness on the hind legs, lameness and symptoms of pain (see p126, Pain). As soon as you notice any signs, talk to your veterinarian and follow his or her advice.

TREATMENTS
• A daily non-steroidal, anti-inflammatory drug.
• Drugs that help promote the production of joint fluid.
• Homeopathic and natural remedies, including substances such as glucosamine, as well as herbal remedies and shark cartilage.

Top: *As dogs age, their muzzles may grey and they may suffer from osteo-arthritis, in the form of stiffness in the knee – just like their human companions.*

REDUCED BLADDER CAPACITY AND BLADDER CONTROL

One of the earliest signs of this may be that the dog needs to go out several times during the night. The dog also begins to lose control over its bladder (urinary incontinence), leaving puddles of urine on its bed or on the floor where it sits or lies down.

Make up special bedding: place a plastic sheet on top of the bed, cover with a thick wad of newspaper, and top with a polyester fur or sheepskin rug. Urine drains down through the rug into the newspaper, leaving the top of the bed dry. Change the newspaper as necessary.

CONSTIPATION

Arthritic changes may prevent an old dog from adopting a normal excretory posture.
• Try increasing the fibre in the diet by including bran or bran biscuits, and/or grated vegetables, and add a tablespoonful of mineral oil as a lubricant.
• Change to a suitable diet prescribed by your veterinarian.

Above: *Musculo-skeletal problems are common in old age. When this occurs, some dogs will benefit from chiropractic treatment.*

INCREASING DEAFNESS

In the early stages, deafness may be difficult to detect, as many dogs adapt quite well. Watch out for the following signs:
- failure to respond to your calls
- increased barking, usually for no apparent reason. This may occur while the dog is lying down on its bed
- barking in an altered voice, usually of a higher pitch than normal.

As your dog's hearing deteriorates, take special care to protect it from accidents. Keep it close to you during walks, and replace verbal calls with physical action – for example, instead of calling it back, go and fetch it.

INCREASING BLINDNESS

During its early stages, deteriorating sight may not be detected. Later signs include:
- the eyeballs appear a bluish colour (cornea affected)
- the eye appears white in the centre (cataract)
- the dog may blunder into the furniture
- the dog is reluctant to go out at night and/or in bright sunlight.

Try not to move the furniture, but protect the dog from danger. A partially or completely blind dog can usually live a contented life as long as it is in familiar surroundings.

SENILITY

Signs are:
- disorientation
- restlessness
- increased demand for your attention
- increased vocalization

Medication is now available to treat senility

▶ CARING FOR AN ELDERLY DOG ◀

Just like old people, old dogs have good days and bad days. You will have to adapt, and be tolerant and sympathetic to the dog's needs. As the situation progresses you will probably need an increasing amount of involvement from your veterinarian, and medication could be neccessary.

To reduce stress on your ageing dog, supply a comfortable bed such as a polystyrene bean bag or sheepskin rug. Supply extra warmth through a heated pad, and don't allow your dog to lie on rough surfaces. Because an elderly dog spends a lot of time lying down it develops calluses on its elbows and hocks. Rough surfaces can cause these to become inflamed and painful, and they may ulcerate.

You could also:
- put comfortable blankets or rugs in its favourite lying places, out of full sun and away from damp areas
- avoid putting your dog out in very hot sun, or into very cold winter conditions
- dress it in a dog coat, even indoors
- protect it from situations in which it is likely to fall: for example, put barriers across steps or stairs, and make sure that it cannot fall from a sundeck
- hand massage your dog's limbs to help improve its mobility
- allow it to take the exercise it wants, rather than what you think it needs. Because its senses of sight and scent are deteriorating,

Above: *Cataracts are common in old age – the eye will appear white in the centre – but most dogs can adapt. Surgery is often a good option.*

your ageing dog can become disoriented, so stay close to it when it is off the lead.

If your dog shows less interest in eating, slightly warm the food or change the diet to something more palatable. Adjust its food intake according to its level of activity. As a dog takes less exercise, it tends to put on weight, and an overweight dog is more prone to heart disease and other health problems. Ask your vet about diets that are formulated specially for various health conditions (see p49, Nutrition). Also monitor how much water your old dog is drinking. If the quantity appears to be increasing, talk to your vet. Take your dog for regular health checks. Booster vaccinations need to be kept up to date, teeth and gums checked and anal sacs emptied. Routine blood sampling may assist with health care.

▶ THINKING ABOUT A REPLACEMENT ◀

As your dog begins to age, you may decide to bring a new, younger dog into the household. You will have to spend a little time on integrating the two animals, but it creates a transitional stage that may help you to cope with the impending loss of an old friend. You may, on the other hand, decide to wait. Nursing an old dog may be enough for you to cope with, without having to spend time with a younger one that needs a lot of attention and basic training. If you are in any doubt, ask your veterinarian for advice.

▶ THE FINAL DAYS ◀

This can be the most difficult period of your relationship with your dog, yet in many ways is one of the most rewarding. This is your final opportunity to repay the love and devotion that your dog has given to you during the happy times you have spent together. If you know what to expect during these remaining days, you will find the inner strength to cope with them.

As your old dog becomes more frail, its reliance on you will increase. Physical contact, and the message of love that it carries, is important, so spend as much time as necessary gently stroking and cuddling your dog to let it know that you are there, and how much you care.

Above: *This old painting of an Affenpinscher commemorates a dearly loved pet.*

▶ MAKING THE DECISION ◀

Sometimes the final decision is made for you. Death may come suddenly, a quick and merciful release from pain and suffering, ending a life from which all the joy has gone.

In most cases, though, there is no natural solution. You will have to make the decision to authorize euthanasia. The decision may come easily, or you may find it very difficult. We witness death on television, videos and films many hundreds of times every year, yet most of us live in a society that does not cope well with dying, and are unprepared for it in 'real life'. If there are children in your family, discuss the situation with them and allow them to express their feelings. Talk about the positive aspects of owning your dog, and explain that however good its health care may be, dogs have a much shorter life expectancy than we do.

The overriding factor in your decision must be what is best for the dog, not for you or your family. That decision will probably be made with the help of your veterinarian, who can play an important role as counsellor and advisor. Vets and their staff understand your grief and sense of loss, but also know that they can end your dog's suffering in a humane way.

THE GRIEVING PROCESS

Grieving is a natural human reaction to the death of a much-loved person or animal. While society has long recognized the need to express it for humans, there has been less understanding of the need to express grief for pets. This situation is changing, though, as we are learning more about the companion animal-human bond that develops between owners and their pets. There are five well-documented stages in the grieving process.

Top: *Bad teeth, a sore neck and a number of other health problems can cause a loss of appetite.*

DENIAL AND DEPRESSION

When you are confronted with the fact that your dog is at the end of its life, you will probably suffer from depression. This reaction will often be subconscious, and is not immediately apparent to those around you.

You may tell yourself that your vet has it wrong, or that things are not as bad as they seem. This reaction cushions your mind against the emotional blow it is experiencing.

BARGAINING

In the human grieving process this involves offering some personal sacrifice if the loved one is spared. It is less likely to happen with your pet, but you may still say things to yourself such as, 'If you get better I promise to take you back to your favourite park'.

PAIN AND ANGER

Your emotional pain evokes a feeling of anger that may be directed at somebody else, such as a close relative or even your veterinarian. It helps you to relieve your feeling of frustration, although this may be at somebody else's expense. Your anger may be directed at yourself, and emerge as a feeling of guilt: 'If only I hadn't. It is at this stage that the support of your veterinarian may be particularly helpful. Negative feelings are not constructive, and need to be replaced by positive thoughts such as 'I'm so glad that I did...'.

GRIEF

By this stage anger and guilt have gone. You are faced with the grim reality that your dog is dead, and all that remains is an empty feeling. The less support you get at this stage, the longer that feeling will last.

If support doesn't come from your family or friends, then get it from another source, such as your veterinarian, a pet cemetarian or a professional counsellor.

ACCEPTANCE AND RESOLUTION

It will take time, on average about three to four months, but eventually your grieving will come to an end. Fond memories will replace grief, and appreciation will replace the sense of loss. You may even celebrate them by obtaining a new pet.

Our pets have a shorter life span than we do, and on average an owner will suffer the loss of a dearly loved pet five times or more during a lifetime. Each time such a loss occurs, that owner will experience a feeling of grief. It doesn't get any easier the more often it happens, for each pet is an individual and the owner grieves individually for it.

Nevertheless, if you understand the stages of the grieving process and know how your family, friends and veterinarian can help, you should be able to deal with the loss with minimum of pain and maximum love.

THE PROCEDURE

The procedure for euthanasia is similar to that used when a dog needs to be anaesthetized for an operation, except that in this case an overdose of anaesthetic is injected into the vein. There is no pain, and the dog loses consciousness within three to five seconds.

You may wish to be present during this procedure. Gently stroke your dog's head as the drug is injected, and spend a little time holding it after it has passed away. On the other hand, you might prefer not to witness the procedure, and would rather say your last farewell afterwards. The choice will be yours.

At this point you will probably feel an overwhelming sense of loss. Don't be afraid to express it. Your veterinarian and the veterinary hospital staff who have assisted will understand that this is a natural reaction.

BURIAL OR CREMATION

If you wish, your veterinarian will help you decide what to do next.

The ritual burial of pet remains is not unusual, and if you don't own a suitable area for this you may decide to purchase a burial plot at a pet cemetery. Prices vary, depending on the size of plot and the quality of casket. Some pet cemeteries include in their price a small inscribed granite marker, but you can also purchase a more elaborate memorial. If you choose cremation, a casket or urn containing the ashes can be returned to you.

You may wish to commission a monumental portrait, a long-lasting and durable photographic image that can be fixed outside on virtually any surface. Many pet cemeteries now provide for after-care of your pet's burial site. If you want to formalize your grief through a brief or extended funeral service, there will be somebody who can help you to arrange it.

COUNSELLING

For some pet owners the lingering grief becomes intolerable. Seek help. You may want to call a traditional counselling service, or contact a veterinary teaching institution with social workers trained to counsel pet owners (these are more common in the United States). Once again, your vet should be able to advise you.

Above: *Dogs left to sleep on hard surfaces or in cold conditions are more likely to suffer from arthritis when they are older. An early sign is stiffness when getting up.*

BREEDING AND REPRODUCTION

▶ A NEW MEMBER OF THE FAMILY ◀

Puppies are adorable, but breeding from a family pet is not really advisable. It is far better to leave this to the experts who have proper facilities and plenty of time. If you do have the time and are really committed, and one family member will be at home all day, then go ahead.

Contact the breeder of your bitch and let them choose a suitable mate. It is not acceptable to find any male of the same breed and use him as the sire as this may result in inferior puppies. It is important to select a male with the right genetic background, a good temperament, of good physical conformation and proven fertility.

▶ THE FEMALE REPRODUCTIVE CYCLE ◀

Most bitches come into season (are in heat) every six months from the age of six to eight months. It is best to breed from the second or third heat. Each heat lasts for three weeks. Signs of heat are vulval swelling, followed by bleeding from the vulva. This lasts for about seven days and is followed by a straw-coloured discharge lasting for another week. There is no visible discharge during the third week. Bitches vary in the amount of discharge produced and some are so thorough in cleaning it up that owners have difficulty in detecting the heat.

Behavioural changes also occur during this time. The bitch becomes friendlier and may hold her tail down and to one side when patted near the tail base. She may also try to wander, and may urinate more frequently. Male dogs can detect the scent of a bitch in heat from long distances and you may end up with dogs camped on your lawn for a while. Keep the bitch safely enclosed during her heat and take her out only on a lead.

The bitch is most fertile between the 10th and 14th days of heat, although there is individual variation. If the dog chosen as sire is close by, then you can visit daily over this time and let nature take its course. However, if the sire is some distance away, it is useful to know exactly when the bitch will be fertile. This can be detected by a blood test, which measures serum progesterone levels. Your veterinarian can advise you on this.

Left: *Making an effort to understand your dog — and carefully managing it — will make having a pet, of almost any breed, so much more rewarding for you.*

▸ MATING ◂

In most cases, mating occurs reasonably rapidly after the dogs are introduced, especially if the stud dog (sire) is experienced. There are instances, though, where the dogs simply don't like each other and mating does not occur. Often this is because the bitch is dominant over the dog. If this happens, and you know that the bitch is definitely at the most fertile part of her cycle, it is better to find a different sire. Mating is usually done in the sire's home environment.

During mating, a gland on the male's penis becomes enlarged, entrapping the penis within the female tract for up to 20 minutes. During this time, the male may dismount and stand alongside or behind the bitch.

Many owners become quite distressed seeing this for the first time, but it is perfectly normal and the best thing to do is go and have a cup of tea for 20 minutes and leave them to it. This 'tie', as it is referred to, occurs in most but not all matings. If it does not occur, it is possible that the mating is still fertile.

▸ MISMATING ◂

There are times when an unplanned mating occurs. If the bitch and the dog are tied together, do not forcibly separate them. Once natural separation has occurred, you must decide how to proceed. You have no way of knowing if the mating will be fertile.

If you are happy to let the bitch have the puppies resulting from this mating, proceed as discussed later.

If you do not want the bitch to have the litter, and you wish to breed from her at a later date, your veterinarian can give her an injection to prevent pregnancy. There may be side effects from this, so talk to your vet about the pros and cons. If you don't want the bitch to have the litter, and you don't want to breed from her at a later date, you can have her spayed once her heat is finished.

Top: *A bitch prepares her whelping area: she may tear up paper or fabric to make a nest.*
Above: *The typical behaviour for four-day old puppies is sleeping and suckling.*

▶ CARE OF THE BITCH ◀

Before a bitch is mated, it is important that she has had a recent health check and has had vaccinations within the last six months. This will help to ensure that the puppies are born with good levels of immunity to common diseases. It is also important that the bitch is treated for roundworms prior to mating and through the duration of her pregnancy. Applied products that are not absorbed but bind onto the lipid (oily) layer on the skin surface are safe to use. Check with your vet about the correct treatment. During her pregnancy, the bitch should be familiarized with the whelping area. Ideally this should include a boxed-off bed area large enough for the bitch to stretch out fully lying on her side and for her to comfortably turn around in. It should be placed in an area that is quiet and away from the mainstream household traffic.

Put newspapers and old towels in the box for her to nest with. Place her in the area with a biscuit or one of her meals for a short while daily.

If she is used to sleeping on a bed of her own, move this into the whelping box and encourage her to sleep there.

▶ WHELPING ◀

The first stage of labour is indicated by restlessness, panting and pacing. This may continue for up to eight hours. The bitch will often tear up paper during this time and make a nest.

Eventually there will be obvious abdominal contractions and the bitch will get up and down frequently and will lick at her vulva. Within 20 to 60 minutes after the contractions

Top: *The Border Collie, an excitable, boisterous and often aggressive breed, is safe and snug with her litter in her whelping box.*

begin, the first pup will be delivered. The puppies are covered with a membrane, which the bitch moves by licking. They are attached via the umbilical cord to the placenta, which is delivered at the same time. The bitch chews through the umbilical cord and usually eats the placenta. She should be allowed to do this. The pups respond to her licking and nuzzling with high-pitched cries. They rapidly find the teats and begin to suckle.

If for some reason the bitch does not attend to one of her newborn puppies, it will be necessary to intervene (see the illustration below).

Have some clean, reasonably rough towels on hand. Make sure your hands are clean, and break the membrane over the puppies' mouth and nose. Try to clear fluid from its mouth with your finger and by holding it facing head down.

Rub the puppy vigorously with the towel until it is obviously breathing and begins to cry. Place the puppy back in the nest near a teat. If the bitch has not chewed through the umbilical cord after 20 minutes, you should tie the cord off with thread and remove the placenta.

If at any stage the bitch strains and pushes for longer than half an hour without producing a puppy, call your veterinarian.

Once the labour is over, offer the bitch some warm milk with glucose (one teaspoonful of glucose to one cup of milk). Leave her alone to rest and bond with the puppies.

It is better for one person only to be present during the whelping – your assistance may be needed – but if you feel that your children would benefit by being present, insist that they are quiet and do not handle the newborn puppies.

THE CORRECT WAY IN WHICH TO INTERVENE IN THE BIRTH PROCESS

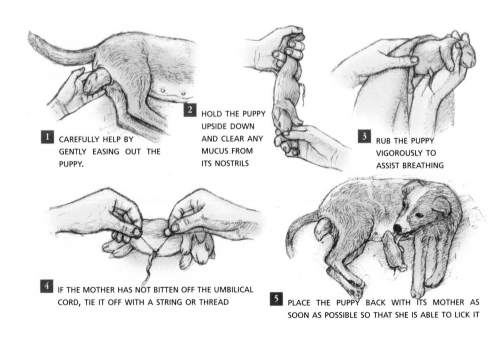

1 CAREFULLY HELP BY GENTLY EASING OUT THE PUPPY.

2 HOLD THE PUPPY UPSIDE DOWN AND CLEAR ANY MUCUS FROM ITS NOSTRILS

3 RUB THE PUPPY VIGOROUSLY TO ASSIST BREATHING

4 IF THE MOTHER HAS NOT BITTEN OFF THE UMBILICAL CORD, TIE IT OFF WITH A STRING OR THREAD

5 PLACE THE PUPPY BACK WITH ITS MOTHER AS SOON AS POSSIBLE SO THAT SHE IS ABLE TO LICK IT

▶ REARING THE PUPPIES ◀

During the first two weeks of life the puppies spend most of their time suckling and sleeping. Feed the bitch up to four times daily during this time and ensure she has plenty of water available. Make sure that she has enough calcium in her diet while she is feeding. If you are using a commercial diet, this should all be taken care of for you. There are special foods designed for the lactating bitch which are also suitable as food for the puppies when they start on solids. If you are feeding a home-cooked diet you will need to add calcium. This can be purchased in powder, liquid or tablet form from your vet.

Most bitches prefer to be left undisturbed during the first two to three weeks after the labour. Take her out to toilet three or four times daily and change the nest twice daily while she is out on a toilet break – otherwise leave her to it unless she demands your company. Some bitches may show aggression at this time, and this is quite a problem (see pp91–2, Maternal aggression).

If the bitch has produced a huge litter and cannot feed them all, you may need to supplement their feeding using a pet nursing bottle and pet milk replacement formula.

A reasonable litter size for a medium to large bitch is six to 10 pups. Anything over 10 may be a problem, although some mothers do manage to rear large numbers successfully. Check that all the puppies feed successfully and have full stomachs. If any of them seem thin and cry persistently, they are probably not getting sufficient food. If you are in any doubt, ask your veterinarian to evaluate the situation. Supplementary feeding of milk and formula is usually done in rotation with half the litter on the mother and half bottle fed at each feeding time (every two to three hours).

At 10 to 14 days of age the puppies' eyes will open and they will become more mobile and start to show early play behaviour. From two weeks onwards they should be offered solid food. Offer this four times daily. Baby

Top: *A large litter may require additional feeds with a pet nursing bottle and pet milk formula.*

cereals may be offered as well as canned puppy food or scraped meat (meat that has been frozen and is then grated and thawed). As previously mentioned, there are special commercial puppy-rearing foods available, which are generally a more suitable option.

The bitch may regurgitate food for the pups – this is normal behaviour and they may be allowed to eat what she produces.

Puppies should be treated for worms fortnightly from two weeks old, using tablets or a suspension. Worming is essential, as puppies become infected with worms before birth. No matter how well cared for, most bitches will carry the larval form of roundworms encysted in tissue somewhere in their bodies. When exposed to hormones during the pregnancy, these larvae are triggered to develop and migrate across the placenta and into the puppies. The bitch should also be wormed at two-weekly intervals while feeding the puppies because she will become reinfected by cleaning up after them (see pp111–22, Parasites).

From three weeks of age it is important that puppies have contact with people, as they need to become accustomed to handling. If you have visitors to the puppies at this time, take precautions to prevent transmission of viral diseases. Ask visitors to remove their shoes and to wash their hands before handling any of the puppies.

It is also important that from two to three weeks onwards, the puppies have access to an area outside the immediate nest in which to urinate and defecate. This area may be covered with newspaper, or it may be a sand tray. If outdoor temperatures are warm, they may be able to have access to a grassy area.

Puppies should go to new owners at seven to eight weeks of age. It is preferable that they receive their first vaccination before they leave. Most vets will give a discount when vaccinating litters and it is very helpful to have a thorough health check done on each one prior to sale.

Top: *The correct way to pick up a puppy: be sure to support its body carefully.*
Above: *Puppies learn from play – their mothers discipline them when they play too roughly.*

▶ PUPPY SOCIAL DEVELOPMENT ◀

Puppies are born blind, deaf and with limited mobility. Even at this early age they compete for access to their mother's teats. In large litters where not all the puppies can feed at one time, the strongest or most determined will do best.

During the first two weeks (neonatal period), senses of hearing, sight, smell, touch and taste develop rapidly.

At around 10 days the eyes and the ear canals open. By three weeks puppies begin to play. From three to five weeks they make positive responses to the approach of any new individual. This is an important time for them to have contact with people. They experience a fear phase at six weeks so this is not a good time for them to leave the litter. A second fear phase occurs at around 14 weeks. Puppies that have been well socialized prior to this will probably not show much change, but in some cases the change in response to new events or strange people is quite dramatic. If your puppy experiences this, you will need to help it by being patient and understanding.

Substrate preference, the selection of a specific area and type of substance for elimination purposes, develops at seven to eight weeks of age. This is a good time for puppies to go to a new home.

In a natural situation, puppies would stay in a family group for six months and often longer. During this time there is constant change in the relative dominance of individuals within the litter. A puppy that is dominant at eight weeks may not be at 12 weeks.

Puppies learn from play. If a puppy bites too hard, the victim will yelp and refuse to have anything to do with the offender. In this way they learn to control the intensity of their play. The mother will also discipline puppies when they behave roughly.

She does this by firmly placing her mouth over a puppy's face to stop unacceptable behaviour, or she may push it onto its side and place a paw on its neck or shoulder. When a human is training a puppy these actions can be simulated to achieve a similar result.

BIRTH	1–10 DAYS	3 WEEKS	5 WEEKS
BLIND DEAF LIMITED MOBILITY	EYES OPEN EAR CANALS OPEN BEGINS TO PLAY	POSITIVE RESPONSE TO THE APPROACH OF ANY INDIVIDUAL	CONTACT WITH PEOPLE CAN NOW INCREASE
6 WEEKS	7–8 WEEKS	14 WEEKS	
FIRST FEAR PHASE: DO NOT REMOVE FROM MOTHER AND LITTERMATES	TOILET TRAINING CAN BEGIN; PUPPY IS READY TO GO TO A NEW HOME	SECOND FEAR PHASE: BE PATIENT AND UNDERSTANDING	

CHOOSING A BREED

Dogs have been selectively bred for specific purposes over centuries. Some have been bred for guarding or shepherding, others for hunting and retrieving, and others simply to look cute and act as companions. They have also been bred in all shapes and sizes.

Although all dogs share certain basic characteristics such as barking, specific sleep patterns and modes of communication, there are differences in behaviour between breeds. These behavioural traits are used as a guideline for pet selection although, between countries, there are differences in the behavioural and physical assessment of breeds. This is due to different gene pools and a particular emphasis during the breeding-stock selection process.

It is interesting that the further removed dogs become from the original wolf-like body type, the fewer signals (such as submissive body postures) are retained and used in interactions with other dogs.

▶ OWNER-BREED MISMATCH ◀

Due consideration should be given to the breed of dog when selecting one to suit your lifestyle. When doing so, it may be useful to consider parameters such as reactivity (response rate and intensity to stimuli), aggressiveness (hostile or destructive behaviour), immaturity (submissiveness and playfulness) and predatory drive (an innate response to prey species).

- Reactivity – Highly reactive dogs tend to be very territorial and may bark frequently. They may also be demanding of attention and will most probably need lots of exercise on a regular basis and continual stimulation.

- Aggressiveness – Aggressive breeds may be ideal as watchdogs or guard dogs but may tend to be very dominant and may not be appropriate for a family situation, especially when aggression is directed towards people.

- Immaturity – Breeds showing high immaturity scores may be very dependent on their owners and, as a result, should not be left alone for long periods of time. They are also likely to be good in family situations.

- Predatory drive – Dogs with high predatory drives are likely to chase, and may kill small animals and/or livestock. In some cases, as previously discussed, this behaviour can even be directed towards children.

Left: *If you live near the beach or a lake, choose a breed that enjoys swimming and can join in with the family's water sports.*

It is important to remember that not every individual animal is going to be typical of its breed. It is important that, when selecting an individual of the breed you have chosen, the parent animals appeal to you. Also visit the litter several times and observe the individual puppies.

GOOD FAMILY DOGS	HIGH-ENERGY DOGS
• Boxer • Bichon Frise • Cavalier King Charles Spaniel • Dalmatian • Golden Retriever • Labrador Retriever • Poodle • Pug • Rhodesian Ridgeback	• Beagle • Border Collie • Boxer • Cocker Spaniel • Dalmatian • Doberman • German Shepherd • Jack Russell Terrier • Labrador Retriever • Springer Spaniels • Staffordshire Bull Terrier
LOW-ENERGY DOGS	GUARD DOGS
• Bichon Frise • Cavalier King Charles Spaniel • Dachshund • Labrador Retriever • Poodle • Pug • West Highland White Terrier • Rhodesian Ridgeback	• Dalmatian • Doberman • German Shepherd • Rottweiler • Schnauzer • Rhodesian Ridgeback

Above: *Dogs with a strong predatory drive such as these Bloodhounds may not make good pets.*
Right: *Dogs need plenty of exercise away from their own property, and lots of interactive play.*

AUSTRALIAN CATTLE DOG

Active, intelligent, quick to learn. Tendency to nip and show strong predatory drive. Territorial. May retrieve.

- **Country of origin:** Australia
- **Date of origin:** 1800s
- **Life expectancy:** 12 years
- **Weight range:** 16–20kg (35–44 lb)
- **Height range:** 43–51cm (17–20in)
- **First use:** Cattle herding
- **Use today:** Cattle herding, companion

BEAGLE

Bright, active, high activity level, moderate to high predatory drive, tends to be dominant. Moderate trainability. Generally not suitable as a suburban dog due to its need for large amounts of exercise and tendency to wander off, following scent. Needs company and is prone to separation anxiety.

- **Country of origin:** Great Britain
- **Date of origin:** 1300s
- **Life expectancy:** 13 years
- **Weight range:** 8–14kg (18–31 lb)
- **Height range:** 33–41cm (13–16in)
- **First use:** Rabbit/hare hunting
- **Use today:** Companion, gun dog, field trials

BICHON FRISE

Good-natured, low to moderate activity level, low reactivity, good with children and other animals but tends to trigger aggression in other breeds. Low predatory drive. Lively and affectionate. Very dependent. Can be highly vocal.

- **Country of origin:** Mediterranean region
- **Date of origin:** Middle Ages
- **Life expectancy:** 14 years
- **Weight range:** 3–6kg (7–13 lb)
- **Height range:** 23–30cm (9–12in)
- **First use:** Companion
- **Use today:** Companion

BORDER COLLIE

Highly intelligent, quick to train, high activity level, high reactivity, high predatory drive but does not kill. Will round up any livestock including birds. Tendency to snap at noses! Not particularly good with children. Best for smallholdings, farms or very active owners. Often reserved or timid with strangers.

- **Country of origin:** Great Britain
- **Date of origin:** 1700s
- **Life expectancy:** 12–14 years
- **Weight range:** 14–22kg (31–49 lb)
- **Height range:** 46–54cm (18–21in)
- **First use:** Shepherd/cattle herding
- **Use today:** Companion, sheep herding, sheepdog trials

BOXER

High activity level, high reactivity, low aggression, easy to train if not in company but can be easily distracted and excitable in group situations. Low predatory drive. Good family dogs if the children are over 10 years of age and the family is physically active. Good guard dogs, vocal about intruders but won't rush in to bite them.

- **Country of origin:** Germany
- **Date of origin:** 1850s
- **Life expectancy:** 12 years
- **Weight range:** 25–32kg (55–71 lb)
- **Height range:** 53–63cm (21–25in)
- **First use:** Guarding, bull baiting
- **Use today:** Companion

CAVALIER KING CHARLES SPANIEL

Low to moderate activity level. Low reactivity, low aggression. Needs company. Breed predisposition to obsessive-compulsive disorders. Good with children. Low predatory drive. Moderate trainability. High immaturity. Good companion for elderly people, as it is happy to sit beside its owners or on their knees for considerable amounts of time.

- **Country of origin:** Great Britain
- **Date of origin:** 1925
- **Life expectancy:** 9–14 years
- **Weight range:** 5–8kg (11–18 lb)
- **Height range:** 31–33cm (12–13in)
- **First use:** Companion
- **Use today:** Companion

DACHSHUND

Moderate activity level. Moderate reactivity. Doesn't retrieve. Low to moderate trainability. Moderate aggression, may be dominant. Not always good with children. Tends to bark and dig. Long-haired animals seem more reserved than those with short or wire coats.

- **Country of origin:** Germany
- **Date of origin:** 1900s
- **Life expectancy:** 14–17 years
- **Weight range:**
  (miniature) 4–5kg (9–11 lb)
  (standard) 7–12kg (15–26 lb)
- **Height range:** (miniature and standard)
  13–25cm (5–10in)
- **First use:** Badger flushing
- **Use today:** Companion

DALMATIAN

High activity, high reactivity, moderate to high aggression, low predatory drive. These dogs have huge exercise requirement and really need to run. Good family dog and guard dog. High trainability. Good for agility. Likes to retrieve. Good with horses and other animals.

- **Country of origin:** Balkans
- **Date of origin:** Middle Ages
- **Life expectancy:** 12–14 years
- **Weight range:** 23–25kg (51–55 lb)
- **Height range:** 50–61cm (20–24in)
- **First use:** Hunting, carriage dog
- **Use today:** Companion

DOBERMAN

High activity level, high reactivity, moderate to high aggression, may be dominant. Good guard dog, loyal to owner and family, may not be good with strangers. High trainability. Usually not good with young children.

- **Country of origin:** Germany
- **Date of origin:** 1800s
- **Life expectancy:** 12 years
- **Weight range:** 30–40kg (66–88 lb)
- **Height range:** 65–69cm (26–27in)
- **First use:** Guarding
- **Use today:** Companion, security

ENGLISH SPRINGER SPANIEL

Moderate to high activity level, high reactivity, moderate trainability and moderate predatory drive. Bred as a gun dog. Retrieves well. Likes water.

- **Country of origin:** Great Britain
- **Date of origin:** 1600s
- **Life expectancy:** 12–14 years
- **Weight range:** 22–24kg (49–53 lb)
- **Height range:** 48–51cm (19–20in)
- **First use:** Game flushing, retrieving
- **Use today:** Companion, gun dog

GERMAN SHEPHERD

Moderate activity level. Moderate reactivity. Moderate to high aggression. Excellent guard dog. May be dominant. Tends to attach intensely to one person but can be a good family dog. Can retrieve. Moderate to strong predatory drive. Highly trainable. Cautious with approaching strangers.

- **Country of origin:** Germany
- **Date of origin:** 1800s
- **Life expectancy:** 12–13 years
- **Weight range:** 34–43kg (75–95 lb)
- **Height range:** 55–66cm (22–26in)
- **First use:** Sheep herding
- **Use today:** Companion, security, police dog

GOLDEN RETRIEVER

Moderate activity level. Low reactivity. Low aggression, very gentle. Moderate to high trainability. Good retrieval skills. Good with children, excellent family pet. Low predatory drive. Likes water. Friendly towards strangers and happy to wander off with someone new.

- **Country of origin:** Great Britain
- **Date of origin:** 1800s
- **Life expectancy:** 13–15 years
- **Weight range:** 27–36kg (60–79 lb)
- **Height range:** 51–61cm (20–24in)
- **First use:** Game retrieving
- **Use today:** Companion, gun dog, field trials, guide dog

JACK RUSSELL TERRIER

High activity level. High reactivity level. Strong predatory drive. May retrieve. Moderate to high aggression. Moderate trainability. May be dominant. Not ideal for suburban living unless with very active owners. Not child tolerant. Enjoys boats and water, has been known to dive for fish!

- **Country of origin:** Great Britain
- **Date of origin:** 1800s
- **Life expectancy:** 13–14 years
- **Weight range:** 5–8kg (11–18 lb)
- **Height range:** 28–38cm (11–15in)
- **First use:** Ratting
- **Use today:** Companion, ratting

LABRADOR RETRIEVER

Moderate activity level. Moderate to low reactivity. Low to moderate aggression, may be a good guard. Good family pet. Highly trainable. Retrieves well. Very food oriented. Low to moderate predatory drive. Usually likes water. Good with strangers.

- **Country of origin:** Great Britain
- **Date of origin:** 1800s
- **Life expectancy:** 12–14 years
- **Weight range:** 25–34kg (55–75 lb)
- **Height range:** 54–57cm (22–23in)
- **First use:** Gun dog
- **Use today:** Companion, gun dog, field trials, guide dog

POODLE

High activity level. High reactivity. High trainability, very intelligent. Can retrieve. Low to moderate aggression. Good with children. Very dependent, may suffer from anxiety-based disorders. Low to moderate predatory drive. Can be very vocal.

- **Country of origin:** France
- **Date of origin:** 1500s
- **Life expectancy:** 14–17 years
- **Weight range:** (toy) 7–8kg (15–18 lb), (miniature) 12–14kg (26–30 lb), (medium) 15–19kg (33–42 lb)
- **Height range:** (toy) 25–28cm (10–11in), (miniature) 28–38cm (11–15in), (medium) 34–38cm (13–15in)
- **First use:** Companion
- **Use today:** Companion

PUG

Moderate reactivity, low activity level as a result of its poorly designed airway. Good-natured, low aggression. Makes a good family pet. Moderate trainability. High immaturity.

- **Country of origin:** China
- **Date of origin:** Antiquity
- **Life expectancy:** 13–15 years
- **Weight range:** 6–8kg (14–18 lb)
- **Height range:** 25–28cm (10–11in)
- **First use:** Companion
- **Use today:** Companion

RHODESIAN RIDGEBACK

Low to moderate activity. Moderate reactivity. Moderate to high aggression. A good guard. Moderate trainability. Does not readily retrieve. Good family dog and good with children. May be aggressive towards other dogs. High predatory drive.

- **Country of origin:** South Africa
- **Date of origin:** 1800s
- **Life expectancy:** 12 years
- **Weight range:** 30–39kg (66–86 lb)
- **Height range:** 61–69cm (24–27in)
- **First use:** Hunting
- **Use today:** Companion, security

ROTTWEILER

Moderate activity. Moderate reactivity. Moderate to high aggression. Not interested in retrieving. Moderate to high trainability. Can be dominant. Good guard dog. Not really suitable as a family pet, better with single owner or couple. Moderate predatory drive. May be aggressive towards other dogs.

- **Country of origin:** Germany
- **Date of origin:** 1820s
- **Life expectancy:** 11–12 years
- **Weight range:** 41–50kg (90–110 lb)
- **Height range:** 58–69cm (23–27in)
- **First use:** Cattle, guard dog
- **Use today:** Companion, police dog, guarding

SCHNAUZER

Moderate to high activity. Moderate to high reactivity. Moderate trainability. A good guard. Dominant, likes to bark. A great companion but not good with young children.

- **Country of origin:** Germany
- **Date of origin:** Middle Ages
- **Life expectancy:** 12–14 years
- **Weight range:** 15–16kg (33–35 lb)
- **Height range:** 45–50cm (18–20in)
- **First use:** Ratting, guard dog
- **Use today:** Companion

SCOTTISH TERRIER

Low to moderate activity. Moderate reactivity. Low trainability. Not good with children. Low to moderate predatory drive.

- **Country of origin:** Great Britain
- **Date of origin:** 1800s
- **Life expectancy:** 13–14 years
- **Weight range:** 9–11kg (20–24 lb)
- **Height range:** 25–28cm (10–11in)
- **First use:** Small-mammal hunting
- **Use today:** Companion

STAFFORDSHIRE BULL TERRIER

High activity. High reactivity. High aggression towards other dogs but usually very friendly and reliable with people. Moderate trainability. May retrieve but not noted for this. Good with children. Moderate predatory drive.

- **Country of origin:** Great Britain
- **Date of origin:** 1800s
- **Life expectancy:** 11–12 years
- **Weight range:** 11–17kg (24–38 lb)
- **Height range:** 36–41cm (14–16in)
- **First use:** Dog fighting, ratting
- **Use today:** Companion

SHETLAND SHEEPDOG

Moderate to high activity. High reactivity. High trainability. A good guard. Good with children. Gentle, sensitive. Low predatory drive. High immaturity.

- **Country of origin:** Great Britain
- **Date of origin:** 1700s
- **Life expectancy:** 12–14 years
- **Weight range:** 6–7kg (14–16 lb)
- **Height range:** 35–37cm (14–15in)
- **First use:** Sheep herding
- **Use today:** Companion, sheep herding

SIBERIAN HUSKY

High activity. High reactivity. Playful. Not a good guard. Tendency to dominate. Often howls. High predatory drive.

- **Country of origin:** Siberia
- **Date of origin:** Antiquity
- **Life expectancy:** 11–13 years
- **Weight range:** 16–27kg (35–60 lb)
- **Height range:** 51–60cm (20–24in)
- **First use:** Sled pulling
- **Use today:** Companion, sled racing

WEST HIGHLAND WHITE TERRIER

Moderate activity. Moderate reactivity. Low to moderate aggression. Will guard. Moderate trainability, can be strong-willed. Moderate predatory drive. Used in dog agility competitions – dogs perform tasks such as running over narrow beams and jumping fences. In America they are used in earth dog trials in which either prey or objects are dug from holes in the ground. Make good family dogs.

- **Country of origin:** Great Britain
- **Date of origin:** 1800s
- **Life expectancy:** 14 years
- **Weight range:** 7–10kg (15–22 lb)
- **Height range:** 25–28cm (10–11in)
- **First use:** Ratting
- **Use today:** Companion

▶ GLOSSARY ◀

Alpha animal: The dominant male or female in a pack. These animals usually assert their dominance with dominant postures.

Arthritis: A progressive disease in mammals characterized by the slow disintegration of the cartilage in the joints followed by the degradation of surrounding bone.

Behavioural medicine: The use of medication to treat behavioural problems.

Binocular vision: The ability to see with both eyes; with dogs, in particular, their peripheral vision is much wider than ours, about 70 degrees more, which gives them a greater awareness of movement.

Boarding kennels: A substitute home for many dogs whose owners are temporarily unable to take care of them.

Breed standard: A written description of what the ideal specimen of a given breed should look like.

Coccidiosis: A disease of animals caused by any one of the four species of parasitic protozoa named *Coccidia.*

Cross-breed: A type of dog produced by the mating of two different breeds.

Dog-sitters: Professionals who look after your dogs on a daily basis at your home during the time you are at work.

Euthanasia: The act of humanely ending, by lethal injection, the life of an animal suffering from a terminal or an incurable disease.

GABA: Accronym for gamma-aminobutyric acid, a biologically active substance found in brain.

Giardiasis: An infection with the parasitic protozoan *Giardia lamblia,* which may cause mild to severe diarrhoea that may be persistent. It occurs worldwide and may affect humans, most domestic animals and birds.

Idiopathic aggression: This type of aggression occurs for no apparent reason. The dog is violent without any provocation.

Kennel cough: Caused by a combination of various infectious agents, including the bacterium *Bordetella bronchiseptica* and canine parainfluenza virus. It is highly contagious and is transmitted through moisture droplets coughed into the air by affected animals; thus it spreads rapidly among dogs that are closely confined, such as in kennels. Hence, the name kennel cough.

Medial canthus: An anatomical term used to describe the inner corner of a dog's eye behind which lies a tear duct.

Neoteny: A scientific term which refers to the persistence of 'puppy' characterisitics in an adult dog.

Neuron: The impuse-conducting cells in mammals that make up the brain, spinal cord and nerves.

Neurotransmitters: Are chemical messengers in the brain. Various brain regions contain their receptors.

Neuter: The act of castration.

Nictitating membrane: A 'third eyelid' which comes across the dog's eye when the animal is asleep and helps to keep the eye moist and protected.

Olfactory cells: The countless cells located in a dog's nose which enable it to acutely pick up scent, especially that of other dogs via glands found on either side of the neck, and perineal area which secrete a substance enabling it to know their social and reproductive status.

Perineal area: The region between the scrotum and the anus in male dogs, and between the vaginal junction and the anus in bitches.

Posture: A term used to describe the head, ear and tail position as well as hair pattern of a dog, attributes which indicate its mood and intention.

Predatory aggression: Aggression shown during the act of catching and killing prey. This response is triggered in dogs by the sight of prey or prey equivalent as well as by the erratic movements of small children.

Predatory drive: A dog's innate impulse to stalk and catch prey, with attributes characteristic of its breeding.

Puppy preschool: Group training and socialization classes for young puppies. Often run by veterinary clinics.

Serotonin: A chemical, secreted by the thalamus in the brains of mammals, which is responsible for feelings of contentedness and calm. It is an organic compound, C10H12N20, formed from an essential amino acid called tryptophan.

Shadow chasing: An obsessive-compulsive disorder in which a dog will chase shadows without end.

Signalling: A method of communication or signalling among dogs that maintains their social hierarchy without constant fighting. A lower-ranking animal's signals to a dog with a higher standing include a lowered head, averted gaze, tail pointing down and wagging, and ears back. It may roll on its side exposing its throat and stomach, signalling complete submission. The higher-ranking animal maintains an upright posture with straight tail and direct gaze.

Substrate preference: A dog selects a specific substance and area on which to eliminate.

Tail biting: An obsessive-compulsive disorder in which a dog will run around in circles biting its tail for excessively long periods of time.

Territorial: A dog's innate drive to protect its territory and that of its owner.

Thyroid: A gland found in mammals responsible for the secretion of thyroxin which controls the metabolic processes in the body.

Toy breeds: Incredibly small breeds or very small versions of a particular breed such as in the case of a Toy Poodle which is the tiniest poodle you can get.

Vaccinations: An inoculation administered to dogs to prevent the development of particular diseases.

Veterinary clinic: Clinic at which veterinary surgeons treat sick or injured animals and perform routine surgery.

Whelping: A term for the birth process.

▶ INDEX ◀

Note: Page numbers in **bold** refer to all illustrated material.

adoption 28, 99
Affenpinscher **158**
Afghan 12
aggression 87–95, 171
  dominance 87–88
  fear 89–90
  food 90–91
  idiopathic 93–94
  inter-dog **93**, **96**
  maternal 91–92
  possessive 90
  predatory 92
  redirected 93
Airedale **20**
alpha animals 63
amygdala 71
Ancylostoma braziliensis 114
  caninum 114
Anubis **11**
aural haematoma 129
Australian Cattle Dog **174**

barking 76, 81, 84, 96–97
bathing 43
Beagle 28, 172, **174**
Bichon Frise 15, 172, **175**
birth 165–166
bitches 49, 50, 53, 58, 163–168
biting 77
Black Hound 15
bladder control 98, 99, 154
blindness 156
blood 147–148
Bloodhound 15, 66
boarding 47
Border Collie **128**, **165**, 172, **175**

Bordetella bronchiseptica 107
Boxer 172, **176**
brain **71**
  microscopic view **109**
breed selection 29–33

*C*anidae 7
canine distemper 106
parvovirus (CPV) 106, 107
canine social system, The 63–64
Canis familiaris 7
  lupis 7
castration 94
cataracts **157**
Cavalier King Charles Spaniel 172, **176**
Celtic Hounds 13
cheese **56**
chewers 100
Cheyletiella yasguri 122
chicken 55
chiggers see also mites, harvest 122
choker chains **81**
Chow Chow 13, **14–15**
cingulate gyrus 71
citronella collar 81
clip-on collar **80**, 81
Coccidiosis 117
Cocker Spaniel 172
comb, double-sided **42**
commands 74–76
constipation 155
cross-breeds 17, 27 see also mongrels

*D*achshund 172, **177**
Dalmatian 76, 172, **177**
day care 44
deafness 156
death 159–161
Demodex canis 122

dental hygiene 41
de-sexing 44, 101 *see also* neutering
destructive behaviour 97
diet, commercial 52
    home-cooked maintenance 53, 54
digestion 55, 154,
digging 98, 100
Dipylidium caninum 113, 115, 118
Dirofilaria immitis 116
Doberman 19, 172, **178**
dog groomers 43
    sitters 47
dog toys, chewable **36**
dog treats 52
Dogue de Bordeaux 19, **36**
domestication 9
dominant behaviour 10

ears 128–130
Echinococcus granulosus 113, 115
eggs **56**
Egyptian Pharaoh Hound **12**
Elizabethan collar **105**
endocrine problems 135
energy 49
English Springer Spaniel **13**, **178**
escaping 101
euthanasia 159, 160
exercise 41
expanding leads 80
external ear infection 128 *see also*
    otitis externa
eyes **136**–137

fats **56**
Fédération Cynologique Internationale
    (FCI) 16
feeding 58, 59
fibre 57
Filaroides osleri 116
first-aid kit 123

fish **55**
flea 118, **119**, 120
Foxhound 28

German Shepherd 19, **70**, 76, 172, **179**
Giardia lamblia 118
Giardiasis 118
Golden Retriever **17**, 172, **179**
grains **57**
Grey wolves **8**, **9**
Greyhound 12, **28**
grooming 42
    mitt **42**
    parlours 43
guarding 84

harnesses **74**, 81
head halters 81
head pain 127
hearing 69
heartworms 116
hepatitis 106
hippocampus 71
hookworms 113, 114
house soiling 98–99
house-training 38, 83
Huntaways **172**
hypothalamus 71

immaturity 171
immune system, The 104
immunity, active 105
    passive (maternal) 104
infectious canine hepatitis (ICH)
106, 107
inner-ear disease 129 *see also otitis interna*
internal pain 127
intestine 133–135

Jack Russell terrier 172, **180**
Japanese Chin 13

joints 141–144
jumping 79
jaundice 138, 148

kennel cough 106, 107
Komondor 15

Labrador Retriever 76, 172, **180**
leather collar **82**
Leptospira bacteria 108
    canicola 108
    icterohaemorrhagiae 108
Lhasa Apso 13, **33**
lice 121
Linognathus setosus 121
liver 55, 138–139
locus coereleus 71
lungworms 116

Mastiff-type dogs 14
mating 164
meat **54**
middle-ear disease 129 *see also otitis media*
milk **56**
mismating 164
mites, ear 121
    harvest 122
    mange **122**
mongrels **17**, **27**, **110**, **126** *see also*
    cross-breeds
mouth 130–131
mouthing 77
muscles 141–144

nails   43
Neapolitan Mastiff 19
neocortex 71
neoteny 11
nervous system 139–140
neutering 24, 99 *see also* de-sexing
nutrition 49–61

obsessive-compulsive disorder (OCD)
100–101
oesophagus 130–131
oestrus cycle 150
oils **56**
old age 153
olfactory bulb **67**, 71
osteo-arthritis 154
otitis externa 128 *see also* external
    ear infection
    interna 129 *see also* inner-ear disease
    media 129
Otodectes cynotis 121

pain 126–127
pancreas 138–139
parasites 111–123
Pekingese 13
PET Travel Scheme (PETS) 47
play-biting 77
Pointer **16**, 76
poison 60–61
    treatment 61
police dogs **84**
Poodle 76, 172, **181**
predatory drive 171
Protozoan infections 116–118
Pug 172, **181**
puppy preschool 73

quick-release collar **79**

rabies 108–110
ranula 130
raphe nuclei 71
reactivity 171
reproductive problems, bitch 150–151
    male 151
respiratory system 148–150
Rhodesian Ridgeback 172, **182**
Rottweiler 19, **77**, 172, **182**

Rough Collie **18**
roundworms 111, 113

Saluki 12
Samoyed 13
Sarcoptes scabel 122
scent hounds 12
scent organs 67
scent 66
Schnauzer 172, **183**
Scottish Terrier **183**
senility 156
seperation anxiety 99–100
Setters 76
shadow chasing 100
Shetland Sheepdog **184**
Siberian Husky 13, **185**
sight hounds 12
sight 68
sinus cavity **67**
skeleton 141–144
skin 144–146
slip-chains 81
socialization 39
soft harness **73**
soft muzzle 77
spinal pain 127
Spitz Dogs 13
spleen 138–139
Springer Spaniels 172
Staffordshire Bull Terrier 172, **184**
standard collars 80
   leads 80
stomach 131–132
submissive behaviour 10
substrate preference 38

*T*aenia hydatigena114
   *ovis*114
   *pisiformis*114
   *taeniaeformis*114

tail chasing 100, **101**
Taxoplasma gondii 116
taxoplasmosis 116
teething 41
temperament 33
Terriers 13, 14, 76
territory 40
Tibetan Spaniel 13
tick paralysis 121
ticks **120**
tongue **67**
Toxocara canis 111, 112, 114
Toxocaris leonina *111*
training aids 79
   advanced 82
   basic 74
travelling 44
Trichodectes canis 121
Trichuris vulpis 114
Trombicula autumnalis 122

*U*ncinaria stenocephala 114
undercoat rake **42**
urinary problems 146–147

vaccination **106, 107**
vegetables **56**
veterinary clinics 103
vomiting 132

water 57
West Highland White Terrier 172, **185**
whelping 165
whipworm **114**
wolf, Chinese 9
   Europian 9
   Indian 9
   North American grey 9
worms 111

yeast **57**

▶ CREDITS AND ACKNOWLEDGEMENTS ◀

Animal Photography / Sally Anne Thompson: 26, 42(br), 46,76, 98, 105, 126, 141, 152

Animal Photography / RT Willbie: 28

Ardea: 175(br), 183(br)

Bridgeman Art Library: 11

Bruce Coleman Collection / Adriano Bacchella: 14–15

Bruce Coleman Collection / Jane Burton: 2

Cogis / Francais: 18, 20

Cogis / Hermeline: 8, 36(bl), 51, 73, 84(tl)

Cogis / Lanceau: 16

Cogis / Vedie: 21, 33

D.v.d Osten: 10, 41, 124

Gallo Images / Ben Osborne: 17(b)

Gallo Images / Tony Stone-David Tipling: 13, 48, 72

Gallo Images: 48, 72

Graham Meadows: 7, 12, 31, 92, 158, 172, 174(bl), 176, 177(br), 178(tl), 178(br), 179(tr), 180, 181(bl), 182, 184(bl), 185

Isabelle Francais: 9, 32b, 65, 90, 91, 177(tl), 181(tl),

John Daniels: 67(t), 84(tr)

J. Theron: 175(tl), 184(tl)

K. Kik: 77

Kelly Walsh: 52, 53, 54, 55(b), 56–57, 74, 77(tl), 79, 80–81, 82, 109, 123

Simon Lewis: 173

Shoot Photography: 6, 22, 29, 34, 60, 62, 70, 83, 86, 159, 162, 174(tl), 183(tl)

Warren Photography: 1, 4–5, 17a, 25, 32a, 36a, 38, 39, 40, 42(tl,tr,c), 43, 45, 58, 59, 64, 66, 85, 93, 94, 95, 96, 97, 100, 101, 106, 107, 110, 118, 127, 128, 154, 155, 157, 161, 164, 165, 167, 168, 170, 179(br)

PUBLISHER'S ACKNOWLEDGEMENTS

Putting this book together highlighted the value of the Internet for the rapid communication of words, comments and images across the world. But despite these advances in communication, this publishing effort still required the usual amount of expertise, time and teamwork. Therefore we would like to record our sincere thanks to the members of the publishing team in Cape Town. We would also like to acknowledge all the other people, whose names are unknown to us, who played a part in bringing this book to publication.